Milady's Guide to
Lymph Drainage
Massage

MILADY'S GUIDE TO LYMPH DRAINAGE MASSAGE

Ramona Moody French

THOMSON

™

DELMAR LEARNING   Australia   Canada   Mexico   Singapore   Spain   United Kingdom   United States

THOMSON

DELMAR LEARNING ™

Milady's Guide to Lymph Drainage Massage
by Ramona Moody French

MILADY STAFF:

President:
Dawn Gerrain

Director of Production:
Wendy A. Troeger

Director of Marketing:
Donna Lewis

Director of Editorial:
Sherry Gomoll

Production Editor:
Eileen M. Clawson

Cover Design:
Dutton & Sherman Design

Acquisitions Editor:
Stephen Smith

Text Design and Composition:
Publisher's Studio

Developmental Editor:
Judy Aubrey Roberts

For permission to use material from this text or product, contact us by
Tel   (800) 730-2214
Fax   (800) 730-2215
www.thomsonrights.com

Library of Congress Cataloging-in-Publication Data:
French, Ramona Moody.
    Milady's guide to lymph drainage massage / Ramona Moody French.
       p. cm.
    Includes bibliographical references and index.
    ISBN: 1-4018-2472-2
       1. Massage.   2. Lymphatics—Massage.   3. Lymph—Circulation.
I. Title: Guide to lymph drainage massage.   II. Title.
RM721.F747 2004
615.8'22—dc21   2003055220

NOTICE TO THE READER

Publisher does not warrant or guarantee any of the products described herein or perform any independent analysis in connection with any of the product information contained herein. Publisher does not assume, and expressly disclaims, any obligation to obtain and include information other than that provided to it by the manufacturer.

The reader is expressly warned to consider and adopt all safety precautions that might be indicated by the activities herein and to avoid all potential hazards. By following the instructions contained herein, the reader willingly assumes all risks in connection with such instructions.

The publisher makes no representation or warranties of any kind, including but not limited to, the warranties of fitness for particular purpose or merchantability, nor are any such representations implied with respect to the material set forth herein, and the publisher takes no responsibility with respect to such material. The publisher shall not be liable for any special, consequential, or exemplary damages resulting, in whole or part, from the readers' use of, or reliance upon, this material.

To my mentor, Judy Dean.
1933–2003

Contents

CHAPTER 1
The Big Picture   *1*

CHAPTER 2
Tissues and Organs of the Lymphatic System   *5*

CHAPTER 3
Lymph Circulation   *19*

CHAPTER   8
Lymph Drainage Massage Principles   49

CHAPTER   9
The Lymph Drainage Massage Session   63

CHAPTER   10
Face and Neck Treatment Sequence   69

CHAPTER 11

Lymph Drainage Massage on the Upper Extremities and Trunk

CHAPTER 12

Lymph Drainage Massage on the Lower Extremities and Trunk

CHAPTER 13

Cellulite

CHAPTER 14

Energetic and Mind-Body Effects of Lymph Drainage Massage

CHAPTER 15

Using Lymph Drainage Massage with Other Treatments

145

CHAPTER 16

Self-Massage Using Lymph Drainage Massage Techniques

149

CHAPTER 17

Closing

165

Foreword

*E*very now and again comes a book that challenges stereotypes by shedding light in a new way. Ramona Moody French's book, *Milady's Guide to Lymph Drainage Massage,* is one of these books. It challenges in a gentle way the stereotypes of the lymph drainage massage (LDM) industry, a rigid system with a strong emphasis on regimen, a focus on pathology, and an avoidance of nonphysical issues, among others. It differs from other books by presenting an empiric approach with simple, scientific explanations of the lymphatic system and fluid movement in the body. This book invokes science to support practice.

French offers this book for all LDM practitioners, not simply those who work over lymphedema and other serious conditions. It is meant for those who practice: estheticians, nurses, massage therapists, and others. It is intended to introduce LDM practice, and it represents the synthesis of many years of practice by French, an author who has also painstakingly researched relevant literature.

The people who perform LDM are massage therapists and estheticians. They are professionals who perform personal services and who are open to learning techniques to help their clients. Clients who need LDM tend to emerge in massage and skin-care practices. Clients get surgeries, have auto accidents, stagnate from unhealthy lifestyles, get depressed, live stressful lives, and on and on. Massage and skin-care professionals mostly work over the subclinical conditions of edema, which respond most gratifyingly to LDM, and impart real help, not to mention beauty benefits, to their clients. It is to these therapists that this book is primarily addressed.

Outside of exceptional medical practices, as in Europe, where LDM is used clinically, LDM is practiced most often in the realms of health, rejuvenation, detoxification, and beauty. As LDM moves more and more into the spa and beauty industries, materials that address issues in these industries become increasingly meaningful.

Milady's Guide to Lymph Drainage Massage is a radical book in that it addresses a couple of "sacred cows": cellulite management and the energetic effects of gentle, nurturing work. Some in the therapeutic massage industry do not feel massage helps cellulite. Some even contend that cellulite does not exist. Practitioners who do LDM, as well as other techniques, feel that cellulite can be managed to a large extent with lymphatic work and lifestyle changes on the parts of clients. Similarly, some in the massage industry and, to a lesser extent, esthetics downplay or ignore some clients' nonphysical responses to LDM. Why? It is unclear. The fact is that the body-mind connection is largely ignored, and that connection is more important and has more therapeutic value than perfect technique can ever have.

Schools and instructors will find this textbook to be a remarkable tool in the classroom. Materials are designed to cover 40 hours of instruction and in-class practice. All materials are designed to be taught interestingly and learned easily. The part of the text covering the physiology of lymph, its movement, and the lymphatic system is so concise, organized, and interesting that it can be read aloud to great advantage.

So, welcome to a holistic view of LDM that is based on practice while its theory is rooted in science. What a book!

Judy Dean, Holistic Health Practitioner
Prescott, AZ

Preface

*A*lthough it was described before the blood circulatory system[1] in the seventeenth century, the lymphatic system has been largely ignored and misunderstood. The greatest advances in lymphatic system understanding came in the twentieth century. With the discovery of AIDS, more attention, and therefore more research, have been focused on the immune system, of which the lymphatic system is a large part. Research into lymphology has increased modern understanding of the lymphatic system, and it has increased the understanding of, and treatment for, lymphedema.

While the term *lymph drainage* was evidently coined by Frederic P. Millard,[2] an osteopath in Ontario, Canada, modern LDM was developed largely intuitively by Drs. Emil and Estrid Vodder in France in the 1930s. Dr. Emil Vodder originally developed the technique for treating sinus infections, enlarged lymph nodes, and acne. He announced his technique to the cosmetology industry in France, and LDM became an important technique for the beauty industry.

Lymphology research and oncology research are related, because lymphedema is often a result of cancer treatment. For decades, however, cancer treatment's effect on the lymphatic system was largely ignored, and little help was offered during follow-up treatment for cancer patients suffering painful and disfiguring lymphedema. Today there is greater awareness of the lymphatic system and lymphedema among doctors and the public, in large part because patients have tried to understand and cure this condition. Many self-help groups for lymphedema patients have formed, and national groups like the National Lymphedema Network[3] serve patients, therapists, and physicians by disseminating information about lymphedema and its treatment.

Massage started as a medical practice in Europe, but, in the United States after World War II, massage grew to include personal growth and relaxation. The human potential movement used massage to develop body-mind awareness. Many professionals today, including physical therapists, nurses, massage therapists, and estheticians, use LDM techniques. This book is for massage therapists, estheticians, nurses, and others who use massage as part of their professions. LDM also helps patients with edema or lymphedema understand the lymphatic system and possibly learn how to perform LDM on themselves.

LDM is used widely in esthetics/cosmetology because it improves the skin's appearance. The focus of esthetics is beauty, but it has always included health, because beauty really does come from the inside out, and health definitely affects appearance. Esthetics journals frequently offer information on LDM's techniques and cosmetology applications. The manufacturers and distributors of cosmetology products offer LDM training. While very effective, the disadvantage of this training is that it often fails to include a great deal of information on contraindications and safety. LDM imparts important physiological effects on the body, but it is not appropriate or even safe for everyone.

Massage therapists long viewed LDM as a specialty involving expensive training in foreign locations and perceived it mainly as medical massage for lymphedema treatment. When I began massage training, LDM was not regularly offered at any massage school of which I was aware, and it was difficult to find LDM teachers. Now, however, massage therapists have discovered that LDM not only benefits lymphedema and beauty treatments, it is an effective tool for body-mind work, stress reduction, and soft-tissue pain reduction. LDM is used in sports massage, which was the first kind of massage to become mainstream, in the 1980s. Also, LDM is deeply meditative and, in the right setting, produces an altered state of consciousness in both therapist and client.

There are now more schools of thought about how LDM should be performed. The Vodder method of LDM is perhaps the most widely known, but since the 1930s others have researched and experimented with various techniques to move fluid out of soft tissues and into the bloodstream. Lymphology is an unusual field in that there is organized communication and support between medical practitioners and researchers, therapists, and patients.

Modern LDM techniques are often simple and easy to learn and just as effective as more time-honored systems. Self-massage methods help patients who lack access to professional therapists or who cannot afford daily professional therapy, which can be both expensive and time consuming. Self-massage is especially important in countries that lack national health systems.

When I was trying to learn about LDM, I found most texts dated, complex, and difficult to understand. Most discussed only LDM's medical applications. Massage therapists, estheticians, and others in related fields know that LDM has many nonmedical applications.

Massage therapists and estheticians have different but overlapping scopes of practice. Because I am a massage therapist, I may mention massage therapists more often than estheticians in this text, but the information applies to both fields. I based this text on material I have used in the class-room over the past 20 years as a practitioner and teacher of massage and LDM especially. This material is meant to be simple for beginning lymph drainage therapists to use and understand. I wanted a book that explains, in ordinary language, the structure, circulation, and function of the lymphatic system and the indications and contraindications for LDM.

I wanted to write a text that makes basic lymphatic system information accessible and understandable for a wide variety of students. I also wanted to create a minimalist approach to LDM that, despite its simplicity, still very effectively moves fluid through the lymphatic system. After years of experimenting in my practice and in the classroom I have devised such a technique, one therapists and their clients can use for various needs and situations. Medical research supports the idea that very simple techniques can increase lymph uptake and movement through the lymphatic system.[4]

In addition to showing me the merits of simplicity, my experience has taught me that massage therapists and estheticians need not learn everything about the lymphatic system and LDM before working on clients. What is important is that practitioners learn the massage technique well and that they understand the indications and contraindications for LDM. It is crucial that therapists and estheticians practice LDM as they continue training. Many who are not seriously ill can benefit from skilled LDM, and therapists can safely work on these clients while continuing to refine their knowledge and their ability to touch. The more clients therapists work on, the greater the therapists' sensitivity, palpation skills, and technique. As they develop their knowledge and tactile skills, LDM therapists should continue to study and take courses.

About the Author

Ramona Moody French has been a massage therapist for 20 years. Her first exposure to lymph drainage massage (LDM) was in a workshop taught by a colleague. She began to use LDM techniques in her practice and to look for other teachers so she could learn more. She also began to observe different techniques for reducing swelling, whether they were LDM or not. French was fascinated by LDM, which has such profound effect with such subtle work. The more she learned and experienced, the more she wanted to know.

In addition to seeking more training and practice, French began systematically surveying the medical LDM literature. Because LDM is the most scientifically researched style of massage, a great deal of information is available.

On a study trip to China, French was very interested to observe the tui na methods teachers and orthopedic physicians at a teaching hospital in Beijing used to reduce edema in injuries. Tui na techniques differed from and were simpler than Western LDM techniques. Essentially tui na practitioners worked from the periphery of a swelling toward the center, patiently repeating the same stationary circle very slowly until they could feel a change in the tissue. These medical doctors explained tui na technique in terms of traditional Chinese medicine rather than the lymphatic system. French began to also practice tui na techniques.

Since her first LDM exposure French has experimented with techniques in medical journals and other sources, developing the principles in this text. Information about the lymphatic system has exploded in the past 20 years, and the field of lymphology is expanding. New information, as it develops, will contribute to changes in techniques and practitioners' understanding of how massage affects the lymphatic system and thereby human physiology and health. Such material has shaped French's LDM experimentation and has inspired the conclusions in this text. Some of these conclusions differ from what is commonly accepted as important in LDM, and French is very interested to hear the massage community's response.

Over the years LDM became a form of movement meditation for French. Success depends as much on being mindful and present as on technique. French found she was not only helping her clients, she was helping herself. Through LDM, French gained the benefits usually ascribed to meditation. She became more relaxed and peaceful, more mindful and centered in all activities, better able to deal with stress. One of LDM's many benefits is its positive effect on the therapist. For French, LDM is a form of meditation with all its attendant effects on life and living. This work became more a matter of "being" than "doing."

While most discussion of LDM focuses on physiologic effects, the technique has a definite energetic aspect. As French's skill increased, she found she could use LDM to access a client's less dense or subtle body, parts of a person inaccessible by the five senses. At that point, French's experience became holistic. For clients, LDM can be a portal to the true inner self. It gives clients the space, safety, and permission to do inner work.

All massage therapists, estheticians, nurses, and others who perform LDM regularly, who are focused on their work and clients, will develop this same deep connection with their clients and will find they achieve more than just physical effects.

Acknowledgments

No one truly works alone. I am grateful to the many people who, over the years, have contributed to my understanding of the lymphatic system and LDM, including my teachers, colleagues, and clients. Many friends helped with this manuscript, especially Judy Dean, who read every revision and contributed to the material on cellulite, the concept of the healing crisis, and the energetic effects of LDM. Robert Leichtman gave insight into the reciprocal energetic effect of meditative work with clients. Bill Mueller, Mariellen Boss, Linda Barufaldi, D.C., and Don Cornwell have been very supportive. Linda Barufaldi and Don Cornwell also edited the text and offered much useful advice. Others who read the manuscript and gave advice included Winifred Golden, Teresa Reynolds-Nead, and Cassandra Tesreau. In addition, I acknowledge my husband, James French, who has encouraged me through every step of the process of producing a finished work.

I would also like to acknowledge the contributions of the following reviewers:

Felicia Brown
Balance Day Spa
Greensboro, NC

Kathy Chism
National Certification Board for
    Therapeutic Massage and Bodywork
Santa Rosa, CA

Beverly May
Massage Therapist
Redwood City, CA

Missy Chapman
York County School of Technology
Marietta, PA

Linda Rice
Grace College of Cosmetology
Middleburgh Heights, OH

Karen Bonney,
Blue Hills Regional High School,
Canton, MA

Karen Wallace,
Grace College of Cosmetology,
Middleburgh Heights, OH

Opal Mobbs
Texas College of Cosmetology
Abilene, TX

Judith Culp
Esthetics NW
Sutherlin, OR

Sallie Deitz
The Centre for Facial, Plastic,
    & Laser Surgery
Bellingham, WA

Peggy Johnston
Champion Institute of Cosmetology
Palm Springs, CA

Sharon MacGregor
Bloomingburg, NY

Text Overview

*B*efore using this text, therapists need a basic knowledge of anatomy and body systems, as well as knowledge of some sort of basic massage, such as Swedish massage. Every effort has been made to explain all but the most basic anatomical terms. Patients with lymphedema who want to use this text to understand the workings of the lymphatic system and to learn how to massage themselves may want to use a dictionary for any unexplained terms.

This text begins with an overview of LDM and edema. This is followed by basic information about the lymphatic system, including its structure and functions and factors affecting lymph circulation. There is a basic discussion of immunity and immune cells. The text discusses indications, contraindications, and basic principles of LDM, followed by a description of massage strokes. Patterns of lymph drainage and lymph node locations are identified. Specific procedures for each part of the body are outlined with photographs showing the locations of the therapist's hands for each step of the massage. Additional information is given about treatment for soft-tissue injury and cellulite. The concepts of the healing crisis and body-mind effects of LDM are explained, as are therapist guidelines. Finally, there are a glossary, bibliography, and list of resources.

The Big Picture

ymph drainage massage (LDM), a gentle, rhythmic style of massage that mimics the action of the lymphatic system, uses precise rhythm and pressure to open the initial lymphatics and stimulate lymph vessel contraction to reduce edema. Edema is an unusual accumulation of fluid in soft tissues that can be temporary and mild or serious, as in chronic lymphedema.

Understanding Lymph Drainage Massage

LDM uses external massage strokes to move fluids out of body tissues and into the lymphatic system. LDM mimics the lymphatic system, employing repetitive strokes at a precise speed, rhythm, and pressure. LDM stimulates the **immune system**, because it helps move stagnant tissue fluid out of tissues and into the lymphatic vessels, where it is transported through the lymph nodes and purified by lymphocytes.

When performing LDM, the therapist moves the client's skin in different directions: lengthwise, horizontally, and diagonally. These movements, which stretch the microfilaments just below the skin that control the openings to the initial lymphatics, allow interstitial fluid to enter the lymphatic system while stimulating the lymph vessels to contract.[5] Fluids are propelled forward through the lymph vessels and away from tissue areas where fluid has pooled. LDM stimulates the lymphatic vessels to contract more frequently. It also appears to make natural contractions more regular.

In addition to improving fluid flow, LDM is very relaxing. The method's slow, gentle, repetitive movements reduce the body's "fight-or-flight response" to stress (the sympathetic nervous system) and stimulate the body's parasympathetic reaction. The fight-or-flight reaction causes the body to tense and to produce hormones and chemicals for defense. This reaction also depresses the immune system while stressing many body systems, including the cardiovascular system. Over time, such stress can cause physical damage. LDM helps to put the body into a parasympathetic state, which slows the heart rate and breathing, relaxes muscles, and allows organs to resume normal functioning.

Although other massage styles, like Swedish massage, can move tissue fluids, they lack the specificity that is the basis of successful lymph work. LDM is very light, gentle, and strictly paced. It does not use long strokes, heavy pressure, such rapid movements as percussion, or pain and discomfort.

Understanding Edema

Edema is a condition in which excess interstitial fluid saturates tissues, causing them to swell. Edema means that lymphatic flow in that area is overloaded.[6]

Edema can be a temporary problem due to a various factors, such as too much salt in the diet, which causes fluid retention, or the consumption of too much fluid. Muscle contraction and relaxation and low-amplitude body movements stimulate lymph circulation. Therefore, a sedentary lifestyle can lead to edema, because there is too little activity to stimulate lymph circulation. Tissue fluids also respond to gravity, so inactivity can cause these fluids to pool in the legs, ankles, and lower areas of the body. In addition, edema can result from such minor injuries as contusions or burns as part of the inflammatory response. Scar tissue can block lymphatic circulation, causing edema.

Edema may also occur over tissues that are stiff due to emotional trauma. Stress and the fight-or-flight response cause muscles to tighten and to remain tight. Massage therapists, estheticians, and others who perform LDM often experience in their clients this combination of tissue conditions, chronic muscle stiffness, and lymph stasis due to stress. This combination can be seen most clearly over thigh and hip muscles and shoulder and neck muscles.

Understanding Lymph Diseases

Lymphedema diseases, which are serious disease processes, are categorized according to their causes. The two types of lymphedema disease are (1) congenital or primary lymphedema and (2) obstructive or secondary lymphedema.

Exploring Primary Lymphedema

Primary lymphedema is due to the congenital malformation of blood and/or lymph vessels. For instance, there may be an abnormal abundance of blood vessels in one leg. In that case, the surplus blood vessels would release more tissue fluids into the tissues of the leg than the lymphatic system could absorb and carry away from the limb. This would cause chronic edema in the affected leg, while the other limb remained normal. In another case, the cause of congenital lymphedema is the lack of lymph vessels in an area. More women than men experience congenital lymphedema disease.

Identifying Secondary Lymphedema

Secondary lymphedema is caused by obstruction due to infection, injury, irradiation, or surgery. In Africa, for instance, **elephantiasis** is a very advanced form of lymphedema caused by a parasite that infects and scars the lymphatics. In more developed countries, lymphedema often follows cancer surgery, which often removes tissue, including lymph nodes, and causes scarring. Radiation therapy scars the tissues through which it passes, hardening those tissues as if they had been cooked.

Knowing Lymphedema's Effects

Lymphedema has serious complications. Because of scar tissue, fluid is not removed from tissues normally. Instead, the fluid stays in the tissues and stagnates. Bacteria can multiply, causing cellulitis, a serious infection that is difficult to heal and sometimes leads to amputation. Chronic lymphedema can cause the skin to thicken, cool, and coarsen and become prone to injury and infection. The body treats proteins in stagnant interstitial fluid as foreign particles, which causes inflammation and its symptoms of pain, heat, redness, and more edema.[7] Chronic inflammation creates a sort of feedback loop in which the inflammation causes tissues to scar, blood vessels to become more permeable and break down, and more fluid to carry more proteins and other particles into the cellular spaces, which cause more inflammation and edema. The gross deformities of elephantiasis show how severe the problem can become.

Patients with lymphedema must scrupulously protect their edematous limbs from injury and infection. Chronic lymphedema is painful and disfiguring, and patients with lymphedema may struggle with depression because the disease limits their ability to move and function normally. Severe cases can render the patients housebound and sedentary.

Working with Lymphedema

Clearly, working with lymphedema is a job for experienced practitioners who have had advanced training and some clinical practice. In clinical practice, under supervision, therapists are more aware of contraindications and the serious problems that might arise in treatment. They gain experience dealing with all the manifestations of lymphedema. Beginning LDM therapists should always refer out a client with lymphedema or work under the supervision of an experienced therapist or medical practitioner.

Review Questions

1. How is LDM performed?

2. What factors can cause edema?

3. What is primary lymphedema?

4. What is secondary lymphedema?

5. What factors or events can cause obstructive lymphedema?

6. Describe some complications of lymphedema.

7. What is the purpose of LDM?

8. What are the physiological effects of LDM?

9. What is edema?

CHAPTER 2

Tissues and Organs of the Lymphatic System

The **lymphatic system** consists of:

- lymph vessels
- lymph nodes
- aggregated lymph nodules
- tonsils
- lymph tissue
- lymphocytes
- lymph
- the spleen
- the thymus

The lymphatic system is connected to and dependent on the blood circulatory system, but the two systems are distinctly different.

Examining the Lymph Vessels

The **lymph vessels**, which include the initial **lymphatics** or **lymph capillaries**, the lymph vessels, and the ducts, form a network over the entire body to channel fluid out of tissues and through the lymph nodes and increasingly large lymph vessels. The lymph vessels finally connect with the cardiovascular system to channel the fluid into the bloodstream.

There are two basic levels of lymph circulation. Superficial vessels drain the skin and the mucosal tissues that are continuous with the skin and that line the digestive and respiratory tracts. Deeper vessels drain the muscles and internal organs. LDM directly affects the superficial circulation of lymph and indirectly affects the deep circulation of lymph because lymph flow is increased throughout the system.

Studying the Lymph Nodes, Nodules, and Tonsils

Lymph nodes, lymph nodules, and **tonsils** are collections of lymph tissue that filter lymph, destroying microorganisms that may be dangerous to the body. Some are in areas where there is more potential exposure to disease-causing agents, such as the respiratory and digestive tracts. There are also collections of lymph nodes in the neck, axilla, and groin. The spleen, a large lymph node located along blood vessels rather than lymph vessels, is considered the lymph node of the blood. Immune reactions can occur anywhere in the body, but the lymph nodes and the spleen are where most action takes place.

Defining Lymphocytes

Lymphocytes are immune cells that are distributed throughout the body in blood, tissue fluid, and lymph. **B-cells** originate and mature in the bones; **T-cells** originate in bone marrow but travel to the thymus, which produces hormones that help to mature T-cells. The thymus is also responsible for immunity in newborn infants. B-cells produce antibodies; T-cells help B-cells and kill virus-infested cells.

Exploring Lymph

Lymph is a body fluid that consists of water, electrolytes, and proteins. Lymph also contains some of the other substances found in plasma, such as ions, nutrients, and gasses, but lymph contains more water than plasma. Lymph is initiated when blood pressure forces plasma out of the blood capillaries and into tissue spaces (the interstitia), where it is called interstitial or intercellular fluid. **Interstitial fluid** bathes and nourishes the tissue cells and picks up microorganisms, foreign particles, enzymes, proteins, and hormones. Interstitial fluid is then absorbed from the tissue spaces into the initial lymphatics, where it is called lymph.

Because lymph vessels are permeable, there is a flow of fluid into and out of the vessels and nodes. Lymph becomes more concentrated as it progresses through the lymphatic system, because water filters out of the vessels and nodes. Large molecules, like proteins and cells, remain in the lymph vessels once they are absorbed from the tissues and are carried through successively large lymph vessels until they are delivered to the blood vessels in the venous angle at the clavicle.

Delving into Initial Lymphatics

The lymphatic system begins in the tissues with the initial lymphatics, which are tiny one-way vessels with closed ends (Figure 2–1). These vessels consist of a single layer of **endothelial cells** overlapping like thin leaflets. These overlapping cells form **flap valves**, little doorways that

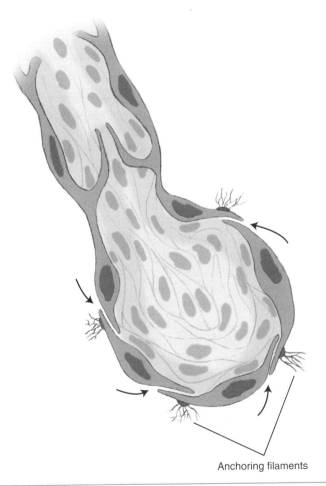

Anchoring filaments

Figure 2–1 Initial lymphatics with anchoring filaments.

open to allow fluid to enter the lymphatic system. These cells are connected to surrounding tissues by fibers. Body movement, including such gross anatomical movement as walking, heart beating, and intestinal peristalsis, causes these fibers to stretch and relax. As these fibers move, they pull the leaflike flaps open, allowing fluid to be absorbed into the lymphatic system.

Initial lymphatics differ from blood vessels. Blood capillaries are permeable, but the size of their openings is fixed and comparatively smaller than the openings in the initial lymphatics. This is because initial lymphatics lack the basement membrane that surrounds larger lymph vessels and blood vessels and gives them structure and strength. This makes initial lymphatics very loosely structured and very permeable. Openings to the initial lymphatics are variable and can widen when there is more fluid in the tissues.

Initial lymphatics also differ from blood vessels and larger lymph vessels in that initial lymphatics lack smooth muscle cells and therefore cannot contract.

Understanding Precollecting Vessels and Lymph Vessels

From the initial lymphatics, lymph flows into larger lymph vessels called **precollectors**. Precollectors are larger than lymph capillaries, have some muscle cells in their walls, and are a little thicker. One to three layers of endothelial cells form the walls of the precollectors. Precollectors carry lymph away from tissues and toward lymph nodes. They are found in almost all tissues of the body, except the brain and spinal cord, bone marrow, and tissues without blood vessels, such as the epidermis and cartilage.

Like the valves in veins, precollecting vessels and lymph vessels are divided by bicuspid valves into segments called **lymphangions** (Figure 2–2). These valves prevent backward movement of the lymph when lymph vessels are compressed. These segments give the lymph vessels their characteristic beaded appearance. Each lymphangion can contract in response to an increase of tissue pressure inside it. As a lymphangion fills with fluid, it contracts, closing the flap valves through which fluid entered it and opening the flap valves leading to the next lymphangion. As the next lymphangion fills with fluid, it too contracts. This wavelike contraction of the lymphangions, similar to abdominal peristalsis, is the most important factor in the circulation of lymph.

Precollecting vessels and lymphatic vessels are most abundant near the inner and outer surfaces of the body, including the dermis (the outer skin layer) and the mucosal tissues (the inner surfaces lining the respiratory and digestive systems.) These areas are exposed to the outer environment and are more likely to contact disease-causing organisms.[6] Lymph

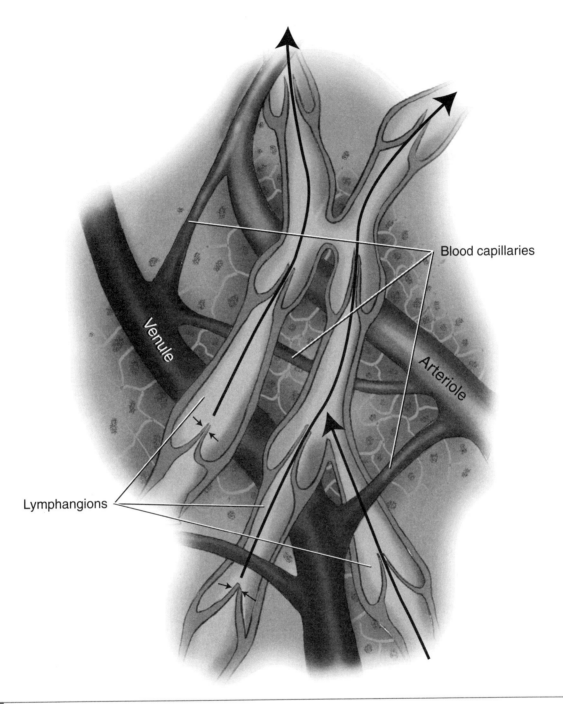

Blood capillaries

Venule

Arteriole

Lymphangions

Figure 2-2 Lymphangion.

capillaries form a dense capillary bed very close to the surface of the skin.[9] This is the layer that is most directly affected by LDM.

Precollecting vessels join to form larger lymph vessels or lymphatics, which resemble small veins. Lymph vessels carry lymph to the lymph nodes, then to the right lymphatic duct and the thoracic duct. Like lymph capillaries, lymph vessels contain smooth muscle cells that contract in response to changes in fluid volume and pressure.

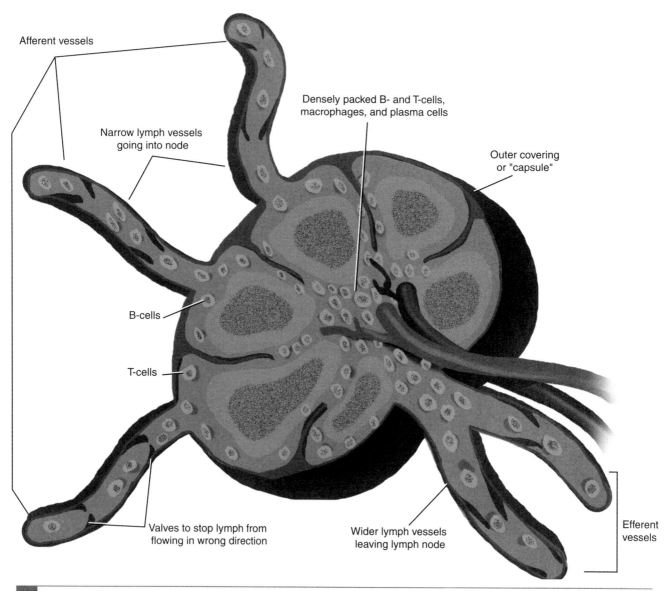

Afferent vessels

Narrow lymph vessels going into node

Densely packed B- and T-cells, macrophages, and plasma cells

Outer covering or "capsule"

B-cells

T-cells

Valves to stop lymph from flowing in wrong direction

Wider lymph vessels leaving lymph node

Efferent vessels

Figure 2–3 Lymph node afferent and efferent vessels.

Lymph vessels that carry lymph toward the nodes are called **afferent vessels**; vessels that carry lymph out of the nodes and toward the lymphatic ducts are called **efferent vessels** (Figure 2–3). Each lymph node has more afferent vessels than efferent, which effectively slows lymph circulation at the nodes. Efferent vessels exit the lymph node at a depression on the side of the node called the hilum. Afferent vessels are attached at various areas on the surface of the lymph node.

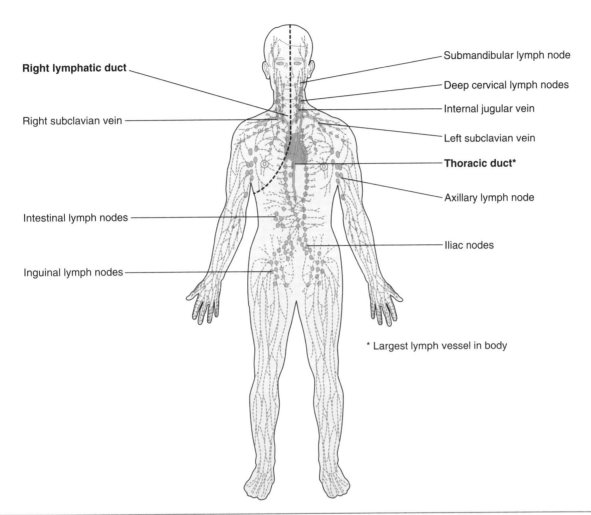

Right lymphatic duct

Right subclavian vein

Intestinal lymph nodes

Inguinal lymph nodes

Submandibular lymph node

Deep cervical lymph nodes

Internal jugular vein

Left subclavian vein

Thoracic duct*

Axillary lymph node

Iliac nodes

* Largest lymph vessel in body

Figure 2-4 Thoracic duct and right lymphatic duct.

Identifying the Lymphatic Ducts

There are two **lymphatic ducts**: (1) the **right lymphatic duct** and (2) the **thoracic duct** (Figure 2-4). Lymph vessels from the right arm and the right half of the head, neck, and chest converge in the right lymphatic duct, which empties into the right subclavian vein. This structure does not exist in everyone; in many people, the large lymph vessels of the right upper quadrant merge and join blood vessels in the venous angle without forming a specific right lymphatic duct.

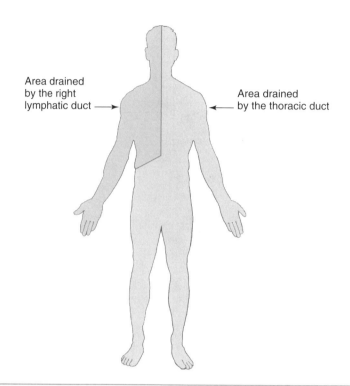

Area drained by the right lymphatic duct →

← Area drained by the thoracic duct

Figure 2–5 Areas drained by lymphatic ducts.

Lymph vessels from the left arm and the left side of the head, neck, and chest empty into the thoracic duct (Figure 2–5). The thoracic duct is located in the thoracic cavity and arises from the **cisterna chyli**, a collecting vessel that receives fluid from the small intestines, an emulsion of lymph and fat molecules called chyle. The thoracic duct empties into the left **venous angle**, connecting to the subclavian or jugular vein (Figure 2–6). Lymph vessels from both lower limbs and the abdominal cavity also empty into the thoracic duct after passing through the lymph nodes.

Discussing the Lymphatic System Organs

The organs of the lymphatic system are composed of **lymphatic tissue**, a specialized type of fibrous tissue containing lymphocytes. Lymph tissue is often called **lymphoid** tissue, but this is not the best term, because the suffix *-oid* means "like." Lymph tissue is not *like* lymph tissue, it *is* lymph tissue. The organs containing lymph tissue include the lymph nodes, the tonsils, the spleen, the thymus, and aggregated lymph nodules in the respiratory and digestive tracts.

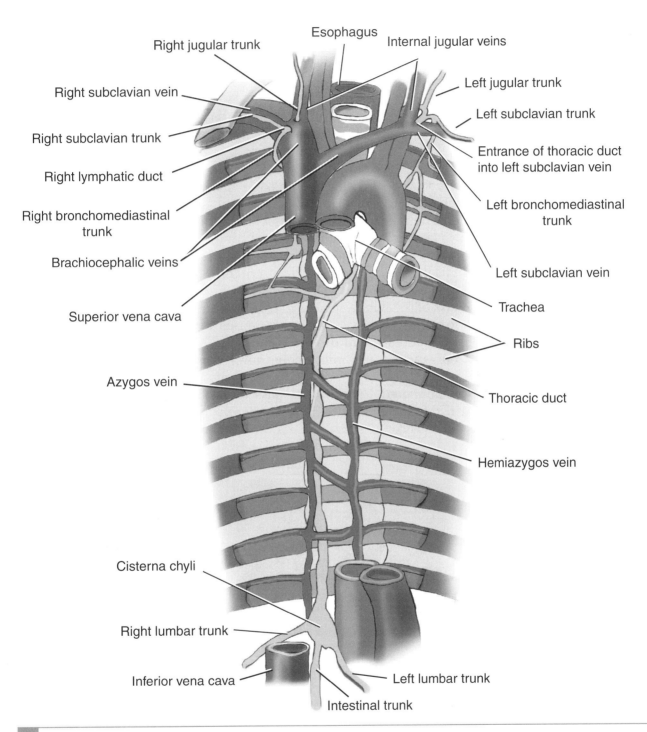

Right jugular trunk

Esophagus

Internal jugular veins

Left jugular trunk

Left subclavian trunk

Right subclavian vein

Right subclavian trunk

Right lymphatic duct

Right bronchomediastinal trunk

Brachiocephalic veins

Superior vena cava

Azygos vein

Cisterna chyli

Right lumbar trunk

Inferior vena cava

Entrance of thoracic duct into left subclavian vein

Left bronchomediastinal trunk

Left subclavian vein

Trachea

Ribs

Thoracic duct

Hemiazygos vein

Left lumbar trunk

Intestinal trunk

Figure 2-6 The venous angle.

Studying Lymph Nodes

Lymph nodes are specialized collections of lymph tissue located along the lymphatic vessels (Figure 2–7). Superficial nodes are mainly concentrated in the inguinal, cervical, and axillary regions. There are smaller groups near the elbows and knees. Deep nodes are located deep in the abdomen, near the lumbar vertebrae, and connected to the small intestines. Some deep nodes are found in the liver.

Lymph nodes are covered by fibrous connective tissue that extends into the lymph node, dividing it into compartments called sinuses. The outer portion of each compartment is called the cortex of the node. The cortex contains dense clusters of lymphocytes called lymph nodules. The center of each cluster is called the germinal center, which is where lymphocytes reproduce by cell division. The inner part of a lymph node is called the medulla. Strands of lymphocytes from the cortex extend into the medulla.

The task of the lymph node is to trap immune cells inside the lymph node and to funnel lymph through the sinuses so that it contacts the immune cells: lymphocytes, **monocytes**, and **macrophages**. These cells destroy microorganisms and microscopic foreign particles that may harm the body. As it comes from the cell spaces into the initial lymphatics, lymph is contaminated. After it has passed through the lymph nodes to be returned to the blood circulatory system, lymph is sterile.

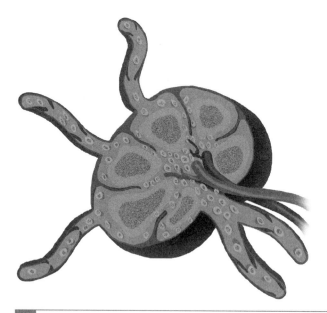

Figure 2–7 The lymph node.

Learning about Tonsils

The tonsils form a ring of lymphatic tissue that surrounds the opening to the digestive and respiratory tracts, an area where harmful substances can easily enter the body (Figure 2–8). Tonsils are lymph nodes, but they lack afferent vessels. Instead of having lymph fluid delivered to them via the lymph vessels, tonsils destroy foreign substances that enter the body through the mouth and nose.

There are three pairs of tonsils: (1) pharyngeal, (2) palatine, and (3) lingual. The palatine tonsils are often removed surgically (via tonsillectomy) when they are chronically infected. Pharyngeal tonsils, often called adenoids, are also occasionally removed when they become infected and obstruct breathing. Lingual tonsils are rarely removed. The lymphatic system can withstand removal of the tonsils, because although the tonsils are the first line of defense for the openings of the respiratory and digestive tracts, those tracts are also lined with nodules of lymph tissue and a rich bed of lymph capillaries and vessels that contain lymphocytes to fight disease.

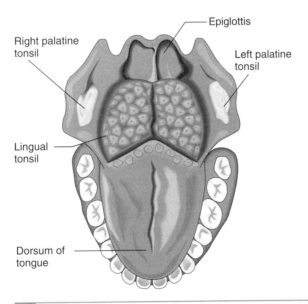

Figure 2–8 The tonsils.

Examining the Spleen

The **spleen**, the largest organ of the lymphatic system, acts as the lymph node of the blood (Figure 2–9). Like other lymph nodes, the spleen traps and manufactures lymphocytes. Instead of filtering lymph, the spleen filters blood. The spleen contains white and red pulp. Blood filters through the red pulp, where dying red blood cells are **phagocytized**, or broken down into parts, some of which the body reuses. Macrophages in the white pulp destroy dangerous microorganisms and foreign substances.

Defining the Thymus

The **thymus** (Figure 2–10) is a two-lobed organ located in the thorax over the heart that is similar in construction to lymph nodes, with a cortex and a medulla. An endocrine gland, the thymus helps newborns and young children develop antibodies and decreases in size with age. It shrinks after puberty but continues to be an active part of the immune system. Immature lymphocytes that are produced in the red bone marrow migrate to the thymus, where they develop into T-cells. The thymus produces a group of hormones called thymosin, which is believed to help T-cells mature. T-cells circulate in the bloodstream and are transported to the lymph nodes via blood vessels connected with the nodes.

Exploring the Aggregated Lymph Nodules

Aggregated lymph nodules are collections of lymph tissue in the mucus tissues lining the respiratory and digestive tracts. These areas include the tonsils, the bronchi of the respiratory tract, the small intestine, and the appendix. Lymphocytes in aggregated lymph nodules respond to **antigens** in those areas (microorganisms or microscopic particles that are possibly harmful to the organism) and create antibodies. The respiratory and digestive tracts are continuous with the skin, and the openings to these tracts, the nose and mouth, allow antigens to enter the body. Aggregated lymph nodules are located to help rapidly overcome the antigens as soon as they enter the body.

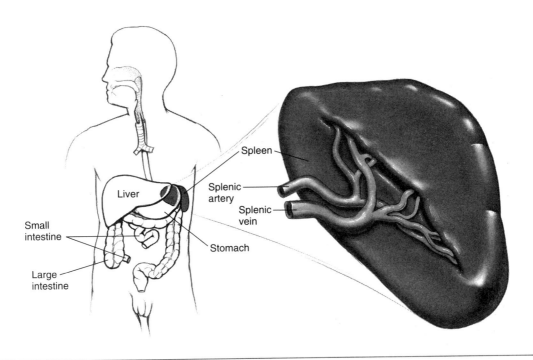

Figure 2-9 The spleen.

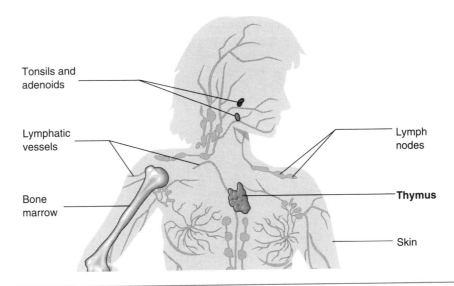

Figure 2-10 The thymus.

Review Questions

1. Describe lymph. What is its source, and how does it differ from interstitial fluid?
2. How do initial lymphatics differ from lymph vessels?
3. What are lymphatic ducts? How many are there?
4. Describe a lymph node. How does it help protect against disease?
5. In which two ways do lymph capillaries differ from blood capillaries?
6. Into which large veins do the lymphatic ducts empty?
7. What is the function of the bicuspid valves in the lymph vessels?
8. The thoracic duct receives lymph fluid from which areas of the body?
9. What is the difference between afferent and efferent lymph vessels?
10. Where are the tonsils located, and how many are there?
11. What is the function of the tonsils?
12. How do tonsils differ from other lymph nodes?
13. Which lymphatic organ stores blood? What are its other functions?
14. Where is the thymus located?
15. What role does the thymus play in the lymphatic system?
16. Describe the location of lymph nodules and the purpose they serve.
17. How do initial lymphatics differ from lymph capillaries?

Lymph Circulation

CHAPTER 3

Lymph circulation differs from blood circulation because the lymphatic system lacks a central pump like the heart. Lymph circulation depends on other factors, like muscular contraction, movement, pressure changes, spontaneous contractility of lymph vessels, and such external factors as massage and gravity. The most important factor in lymph circulation is the **lymphatic pump**, the rhythmic, wavelike contractions of the lymphangions. Unlike blood circulation, lymph circulation is not continuous in all parts of the body at all times.

Lymph circulation involves two distinct steps or stages:

1. lymph absorption into the initial lymphatics and capillaries
2. propulsion of lymph through the network of contractile lymphatic vessels

Beginning Lymph Circulation

The lymphatic system drains all regions of the body. This drainage begins in the cell spaces (**interstitia**) with initial lymphatics, very tiny vessels with closed ends that differ widely from blood vessels. Blood vessels have a well-defined **basement membrane**, an outer wall of connective tissue that gives them structure and resilience. These blood vessel membranes are fenestrated, or honeycombed with windows, through which plasma, proteins, and red blood cells escape from the blood to the cell spaces (interstitia) in the body's various tissues.

Initial lymphatics, in contrast, lack a basement membrane. Because of this, proteins and other components of tissue fluid can enter the lymphatic system easily. They enter through gaps between endothelial cells in the initial lymphatics. The endothelial cells of the initial lymphatics resemble leaves and are connected to surrounding structures by microfilaments. As tissue fluid pressure increases, the gaps between the endothelial cells widen. This allows tissue fluid, with its components, to enter the lymphatics.[10] Body movements like walking, yawning, and stretching, which cause the skin to move, trigger the stretch reflex of the initial lymphatics. The microfilaments that connect the initial lymphatics to surrounding tissues stretch and relax as the skin moves. As the microfilaments stretch and relax, they tug on the endothelial cells in the initial lymphatics, pulling them open and allowing tissue fluid to flow in.

Body movements; such local-area movements as abdominal peristalsis, respiration, arterial pulse; and contractions of local muscles all stimulate lymph circulation. These factors cause the overlapping cells of the initial lymphatics to pull open and stimulate the lymph vessels to contract.

Lymph circulation is also affected by local fluid dynamics. As the volume of fluid in the tissues increases, it fills the spaces between the tissue cells and moves them farther apart. Also, as the volume of fluid in the tissues increases, pressure increases. Fluid tends to move from areas with more pressure to areas with less pressure. Blood pressure forces fluid out of blood vessels, increasing tissue pressure. As tissue pressure increases, the endothelial cells that cover the openings to the initial lymphatics move apart and fluid can enter the lymphatics, increasing fluid pressure and volume inside them (Figure 3–1).[11]

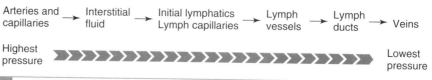

Figure 3-1 Pressure gradient.

Moving into Spontaneous Contraction

From the initial lymphatics, lymph moves into larger lymph capillaries, where intrinsic contractions in the walls of the lymphatics (the lymphatic pump) propel lymph forward, toward the lymphatic ducts.[12] The spontaneous contraction of the lymphatic vessels is due to the increased pressure of the lymphatic fluid.[13] Called the lymphatic pump, these contractions start in the lymphangions next to the initial lymphatics and spread from one to the next. Fluid always moves toward the thoracic duct or the right lymphatic duct. The contractions, similar to abdominal peristalsis, are stimulated by an increase in pressure inside the lymphatic capillaries and vessels (Figure 3–2).

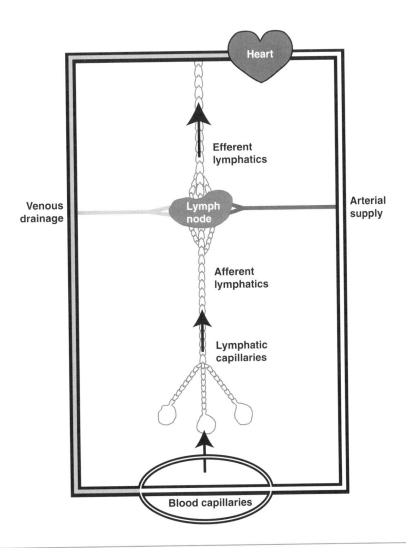

Figure 3–2 Relationship of lymph circulation to blood circulation.

Contractions of the lymphatics are not coordinated with the heart or breath rate[14] but are related to factors in the lymphatic system. Lymphatic contractions start and stop depending on whether the pressure inside the lymphangions exceeds or falls below certain levels. When pressure in the tissues becomes too great, lymph circulation in the area stops and edema develops. Edema is a sign that lymph circulation has decreased or stopped in the area.

Advancing to Skeletal Muscle Contraction

When exercising, lymphatic circulation inside the muscle increases up to 15 times the resting rate. Exercise has the effect of scrubbing the muscles clean. At first, the lymphatic fluid from the muscles is full of proteins, dead red blood cells, and waste material from the muscle cells. As exercise continues, the muscles alternately contract and relax, propelling lymph through the vessels and pulling fluid from the muscle tissues. Gradually, the lymph contains fewer and fewer such particles.[15] The fluid that is removed from the muscles via the lymphatic system is replaced with more fluid from local blood vessels, containing nutrients for muscle cells. However, vigorous exercise that stimulates lymph circulation in muscles is only a small part of the entire lymph circulation of the body. Many lymph vessels are located in the skin and in tissues contiguous with the skin, such as the digestive and respiratory tracts, and the contraction of skeletal muscles does not affect these superficial vessels directly.

Moving to Pressure Changes in the Thorax

During inhalation, the thoracic duct is squeezed, pushing fluid forward, toward the venous angle, and creating a partial vacuum in the duct. During exhalation, fluid is pulled from lymphatic vessels into the thoracic duct to fill the vacuum created by inhalation. Other natural movements inside the body, such as abdominal peristalsis and the beating of the heart, affect lymph vessels and stimulate lymph movement. Pressure inside the chest cavity is less than atmospheric pressure outside the body. This creates a slight vacuum in the chest cavity that helps draw lymph into the thoracic duct.

Advancing to Gentle Body Movements

Low-amplitude body movements, such as walking 40 paces per minute, and such natural movements as blinking, yawning, sneezing, and stretching, tend to empty lymphatics in the chest and abdomen, which then draw in fluid from the lymphatics in the peripheries.[16] Inactivity can contribute to lymph stasis (edema). Then, tissue fluid tends to pool in lower regions of the body in response to gravity. One example is the painful swollen legs experienced by many who take long international flights during which they must sit in one place for hours at a time.

Lymph circulation slows during rest. Stretching and yawning upon awakening help to start lymph circulation.

Working with Variations in Internal Pressure

Plasma is forced out of blood capillaries because blood pressure is greater than the pressure in the surrounding tissues. Increased fluid volume in the cellular spaces of surrounding tissues (interstitia) causes cells to move apart, straining the microscopic fibers that connect the endothelial cells of the initial lymphatics to tissue cells. The pull on the microfilaments causes the endothelial cells to open like flaps, allowing tissue fluid to enter the initial lymphatics. The pressure of the accumulating fluid in the initial lymphatics forces lymph through one-way valves and into larger lymph capillaries.

Accommodating External, Mechanical Factors

Massage and passive movement increase lymph flow and the rate of contractions of the lymphatic vessels.[17] Massage mechanically moves fluid, like squeezing water through a tube. It also stimulates the lymph vessels to contract, starting the lymphatic pump so that lymph circulation will continue on its own.

Passive movement, which is when the therapist helps the client move the arms and legs, also helps to stimulate lymph circulation, a real benefit to those immobilized by injury and paralysis. Similarly, limb elevation allows gravity to function so that lymph flows away from the limb.[18] To be most effective, the arms and legs must be properly elevated. If the knees are elevated but the ankles and feet are not, lymph from the lower leg will not drain as effectively. With the client lying in a supine position, the ankles must be propped up slightly higher than the knees, which must be a little higher than the hip joint. The hip joint should be only slightly flexed to prevent compressing lymphatics in the region of the joint. Similarly, when elevating the arm, the hand must be slightly higher than the elbow, which in turn must be slightly higher than the shoulder.

Review Questions

1. List at least three factors that affect lymph circulation.

2. What are the two stages of lymph circulation?

3. What is the primary difference between the lymph and blood circulatory systems?

4. What is the lymphatic pump?

5. Describe the effects of exercise on lymph circulation.

6. Which factors can hinder lymph circulation?

7. The lymphatic system is part of what larger system?

CHAPTER 4

Functions of the Lymphatic System

The lymphatic system has a number of important functions.[19] It helps balance fluid and distribute immune cells throughout the body to maintain health and defend against disease. The lymphatic system also rids tissues of excess proteins and toxins and carries digested fat from the intestines to the blood vessels. It helps to repair damage in injured tissues. The lymphatic system can also regenerate and even develop new lymph nodes in areas of chronic infection.

Identifying Basic Lymphatic System Functions

The lymphatic system is the first line of defense against disease on a cellular level. The lymphatic system helps to transport immune cells throughout the body. Also, lymph nodes filter lymph and the spleen filters blood. These organs contain lymphocytes that can recognize and destroy microorganisms and such foreign substances as pesticides, which harm the organism. The success of the lymphatic system depends on the ability of the immune cells to differentiate between cells that belong to the body and invaders that do not. It also depends on the ability of immune cells to create antibodies. Immune cells create antibodies for each disease organism they encounter. For the rest of a person's life, the immune system will recognize and destroy those organisms each time they invade.

The lymphatic system helps to maintain a healthy balance of fluid volume and pressure in both the tissues and the cardiovascular system. Fluid is removed from tissues and returned to blood vessels continuously, helping to maintain tissue fluid volume, blood volume, and blood pressure. A large volume of fluid washes in and out of blood into the body's tissues every day. That fluid, which is basically plasma and contains proteins, lymph cells, red blood cells, electrolytes, and so on, washes the spaces between tissue cells, picking up microorganisms, microscopic particles, and metabolic waste from cells. About 90 percent of that fluid is absorbed back into the bloodstream through blood capillaries, which are permeable. The remaining 10 percent, about three liters,[20] enters the lymphatic capillaries and passes through the lymphatic system before returning to the blood via the subclavian veins.

Continuing with Lymphatic System Functions

Although most of the fluid that filters out of blood vessels into tissues is reabsorbed into the bloodstream, large molecules and cells are not reabsorbed. The openings in blood capillaries are relatively small compared to the openings in the initial lymphatics and lymph capillaries. It falls to the lymphatic system then to return proteins and other macromolecules to the bloodstream. Left in the tissues, proteins can trigger an inflammatory response and the side effects of pain and swelling and scar tissue. Eventually, protein buildup in tissues can be life threatening, so this function of the lymphatic system is vital. The lymphatic system also absorbs foreign microorganisms and particles from tissues and passes all these substances through the lymph nodes, where they are destroyed before the lymph returns to the bloodstream.

The lymphatic system transports fats from the small intestines to the bloodstream through the lymphatics and the thoracic duct. Special lymph vessels called **lacteals** are located in the lining of the small intestine. Digested fats enter the lacteals and pass through the lymph vessels into the veins near the heart. Lymph passing through these vessels, called **chyle**, has a milky appearance because of its fat content.

The lymphatic system also helps to repair the damage from injured tissues. When there is an injury to tissue, such as the skin or a muscle, chemicals from the damaged cells cause inflammation. Blood circulation in the area increases, and capillaries become more permeable. More fluid is released into the damaged area, bringing with it immune cells and fibers that start to wall off the area and destroy any dangerous microorganisms. The pressure difference between the fluid-filled tissues and the lymphatic vessels creates a slight vacuum that pulls debris from the injury, including dead cells, microorganisms, and foreign particles, into the initial lymphatics and eventually to the lymph nodes, where it is destroyed.

Differentiating the Lymphatic System

One of the amazing abilities of the lymphatic system, only recently recognized and not yet studied in depth, is its amazing powers of regeneration. The sprouting of new lymph capillaries in areas where lymph flow has been disrupted has been observed, as well as the growth of new lymph nodes in areas of chronic infection. Apparently, the growth of new lymph nodes along deep lymph vessels in the extremities occurs when normal lymph nodes are scarred and damaged by chronic infection.[21]

The difficulty of studying the lymphatic system in living persons has contributed to slow progress in understanding the system. However, recent developments like magnetic resonance imaging (MRI) and microsurgical techniques, as well as the demand from lymphedema patients for more research, have contributed to knowledge of the lymphatic system and will ease continued research.[22]

Review Questions

1. What are the main functions of the lymphatic system?

2. Why is it important that proteins are removed from tissues, and why are the blood vessels unable to absorb proteins from tissues?

3. How does dietary fat enter the bloodstream and the heart?

4. What role does the lymphatic system play when there is an injury to a tissue like the skin or muscles?

5. What role does the lymphatic system play when someone is exposed to a disease-causing microorganism?

6. How does the lymphatic system affect blood volume?

7. What is the most important function of the lymphatic system?

Immunity

CHAPTER

*I*mmunity is the body's ability to resist damage from microorganisms and other foreign substances, like harmful chemicals. The human body has **nonspecific immunity** and **specific immunity** systems to defend against microorganisms and harmful substances. Nonspecific immunity is innate, but specific immunity, which must be **acquired**, depends on the ability of immune cells to produce antibodies.

Exploring Nonspecific Immunity

Nonspecific immunity or "innate resistance" includes mechanical methods of resistance, chemicals, the inflammatory response, and macrophages, all of which provide barriers to foreign substances. Humans are born with nonspecific mechanisms to defend against disease.

Researching Mechanical Methods of Resistance

Mechanical processes of resistance prevent microorganisms from entering the body, or they remove microorganisms from the body. For example, the cells of the dermis and epidermis create a barrier that prevents microorganisms from entering the body. The acidity and high fat content of skin contribute to this process by inhibiting the growth of microorganisms. Another example is the sticky mucus produced by the mucous membranes. This mucus traps microorganisms and moves them out of the body. Tears, saliva, and urine wash away microorganisms, while nasal hairs filter air during inhalation. The cilia of the upper respiratory tract sweep microorganisms toward the digestive tract where they are destroyed by acid in the stomach. All these entities, without differentiating between bacteria and viruses, react to invaders in the same way.

Reviewing Chemical Resistance

Chemical resistance includes nonspecific antiviral and antibacterial substances produced by the body. Some chemicals on the surfaces of cells destroy microorganisms or prevent their entry into cells. Lysozyme in tears and saliva, sebum on skin, and mucus on the mucous membranes are such chemicals. Interferon protects cells against viral infections by preventing virus replication.

Identifying the Inflammation Response

The inflammatory response (Figure 5–1) occurs when injuries, infections, poisons, and the like damage tissues. **Inflammation** is characterized by redness, heat, swelling, and pain. Increased blood flow to the injured area causes the typical symptoms of redness and heat. So that more fluid is forced into the local tissues, chemicals released by injured cells cause vasodilation and increased permeability of local blood vessels. The

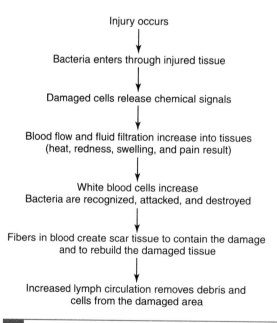

Injury occurs

↓

Bacteria enters through injured tissue

↓

Damaged cells release chemical signals

↓

Blood flow and fluid filtration increase into tissues
(heat, redness, swelling, and pain result)

↓

White blood cells increase
Bacteria are recognized, attacked, and destroyed

↓

Fibers in blood create scar tissue to contain the damage
and to rebuild the damaged tissue

↓

Increased lymph circulation removes debris and
cells from the damaged area

Figure 5–1 The inflammatory process.

pressure of the fluid on nerve receptors causes swelling (edema) and pain. The chemical signals released by injured cells also attract **leukocytes**, which can move toward tissue damage, in a process called chemotaxis. There the leukocytes begin to destroy invading cells, foreign particles, and dead or damaged cells.

The first cells to reach a damaged area are **neutrophils**, which immediately begin destroying invading cells. These are followed by macrophages. Macrophages are monocytes that escape the bloodstream into the tissues and grow. They are **phagocytes**, which means they destroy invading cells by engulfing them and breaking them into particles. Phagocytosis is the process by which phagocytes digest and break down foreign cells.

With the immune cells, fibroblasts migrate to the area of injury and begin to build scar tissue to isolate the injured tissues from healthy tissues and to rebuild the damaged tissues.

As the local lymphatic capillaries begin absorbing tissue fluid, red blood cells (**erythrocytes**), and proteins spilled from damaged blood vessels, lymphatic circulation increases. The local lymphatics absorb interstitial fluid, as well as dead or damaged cells, invading cells, and foreign particles, bringing them into contact with more immune cells in the lymph nodes.

Understanding Specific Immunity

While nonspecific defenses of the body defend against all attackers in the same way, specific immunity defenses of the immune system recognize and destroy specific foreign microorganisms. Specific immunity depends on exposure to antigens and disease-causing cells and on antibody production. In a lifetime, the body's approximately 2 trillion lymphocytes can produce 100 million trillion antibodies, each targeted at a different invading microorganism. Antibodies are developed after the body is exposed to a foreign substance for the first time. They remain in the system and can remember the foreign substance and attack it more quickly on next exposure. One example of this activity is the immunity that results from certain childhood diseases, like mumps, measles, and chicken pox.

A very important factor in specific immunity is the body's ability to recognize self-cells and not-self cells and to destroy only the not-self cells (invading diseases). **Autoimmune diseases** occur when the body becomes confused recognizing foreign cells and the immune system starts to attack self-cells as if they were foreign invaders.

Studying Acquired Immunity

Antibody-based immunity must be acquired as the organism is exposed to a multitude of attacking foreign microorganisms over a lifetime.

1. **Active immunity** or natural acquired immunity results from everyday exposure to antigens against which the body's immune system responds. As humans age, they develop more and more antibodies to different kinds of microorganisms, develop better resistance, and therefore fall ill less often than children.

2. Active artificial immunity results from deliberate exposure to an antigen by means of a vaccine. Weak or dead disease-causing microorganisms are injected and the body develops antibodies that recognize these microorganisms quickly when again exposed to them.

3. **Passive immunity** or natural immunity refers to the transfer of **antibodies** from a mother to her fetus or baby through the umbilical cord during gestation and through nursing. This helps to protect infants and children until they develop their own antibodies.

4. Passive artificial immunity is the transfer of antibodies from an animal or another person to a person requiring immunity. This medical procedure helps those with impaired immune systems who are producing too few antibodies.

Categorizing Cells

Identifying White Blood Cells

The purpose of the lymphatic system is to protect the body against the harmful effects of invading microorganisms, poisons, and dead or dying cells. The lymphatic system has its own cells for this purpose. It consists of stationary cells, which make up the tissue of lymph organs, and moving cells, which migrate throughout the body by means of body fluids: plasma, interstitial fluid, and lymph. As a group, the moving cells are called white blood cells, or leukocytes.

White blood cells or leukocytes are formed in red bone marrow and reproduce in blood and lymph tissue. After leaving the bone marrow through the blood vessels, these cells enter tissues and eventually filter into the lymphatic system. There are five types of leukocytes, each with specific functions.

Examining Neutrophils

Neutrophils are usually the first cells to reach damaged areas, attracted by chemotaxis. Neutrophils ingest bacteria and other substances through phagocytosis. After ingesting only a few microorganisms, neutrophils die readily, creating pus. Pus is dead neutrophils. Neutrophils compose about 60 to 70 percent of leukocytes in the body.

Distinguishing Monocytes and Macrophages

Monocytes are immature macrophages that travel in blood and lymph. They can pass through the walls of the blood and lymphatic system and mature into macrophages, about five times larger than monocytes. Macrophages, phagocytes that travel to damaged tissue after neutrophils, are responsible for most of the activity in the later stages of infection. Macrophages clean up dead neutrophils and other cellular debris, as well as destroy microorganisms and foreign substances. They destroy many more cells before dying than do neutrophils, and they may be found in such uninfected tissues as the skin, mucous membranes, blood and lymphatic vessels, lymph nodes, and the spleen, where they phagocytize microorganisms before they can cause damage or reproduce. Macrophages do not produce antibodies but are part of the nonspecific immune system.

Understanding Basophils

Basophils release histamine, which promotes inflammation. Basophils account for about 1 percent of leukocytes. Mast cells are structurally similar to basophils and do similar work in the immune system, promoting the inflammatory response and responding to allergens.

Defining Eosinophils

Eosinophils release chemicals that reduce inflammation. Eosinophils account for about 1 to 4 percent of leukocytes.

Exploring Natural Killer Cells

Natural killer (NK) cells are a type of leukocyte produced in red bone marrow, composing about 1 to 3 percent of all lymphocytes. NK cells do not exhibit specificity or memory but recognize and destroy a general class of cells, such as tumor cells.

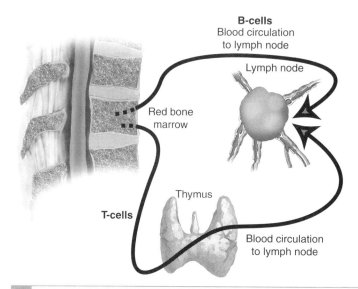

Figure 5–2 Origins of B- and T-cells.

Delving into B- and T-Lymphocytes

B- and T-lymphocytes produce antibodies and other, similar chemicals responsible for destroying microorganisms, particularly viruses (Figure 5–2). Lymphocytes contribute to allergic reactions, graft and transplant rejections, tumor control, and immune system regulation. Lymphocytes account for 20 to 30 percent of leukocytes.

B- and T-lymphocytes originate in red bone marrow. B-cells mature in bone marrow, but T-cells travel to the thymus first, where they mature and are distributed. There are about five T-cells for every B-cell, and both cells circulate constantly through the blood and lymph, although they remain most of the time in lymph organs. B-cells produce antibodies and protect against bacteria, toxins, and viruses outside of cells. T-cells help B-cells and kill cells containing viruses and tumor cells.

Review Questions

1. How does nonspecific immunity differ from specific immunity?
2. Specific immunity depends on what two factors?
3. What is an antibody?
4. What is an antigen?
5. How does inflammation protect the body from disease?
6. In what four ways can specific immunity be acquired?
7. Give two examples of nonspecific immunity.

Edema

Edema is a condition in which excess interstitial fluid saturates tissues, causing swelling. Edema means that lymphatic flow in that area is overloaded.[23] When lymphatic function is overloaded, it is either because the load is too great (the amount of fluid in the tissues exceeds the capacity of the lymphatics), or function has been lost (e.g., lymph vessels are damaged or missing, lymph nodes may have been removed, or scar tissue may be blocking lymph circulation).

Understanding Edema Basics

Edema can be a simple and temporary problem due to various factors, such as too much salt in the diet, which causes fluid retention, or too much fluid. A sedentary lifestyle can lead to edema, because there is too little activity to stimulate lymph circulation. Lymph circulation is stimulated by muscle contraction and relaxation and by low-amplitude body movements. When the body is still and there is little activity, lymph circulation decreases and fluid that would normally absorb into the lymphatic system instead pools in the interstitia or tissue spaces. Tissue fluids also respond to gravity, so inactivity can cause these fluids to pool in the legs, ankles, and lower areas of the body.

As part of the inflammatory response, edema can also result from such minor injuries as contusions or burns. Injured tissue cells send chemical signals that increase local blood flow and make the blood vessels more permeable so more fluid filters out into the damaged area, causing swelling. Scar tissue that develops after an injury can block lymphatic circulation, causing edema. In fact, experienced massage therapists often observe small edematous areas on their clients' bodies that coexist with scar tissue and damage from previous injuries. For instance, many people who have sprained their ankles, even years before, will have chronic swelling around the injured ankles.

Edema may also occur over tissues that are stiff due to emotional trauma. Stress and the fight-or-flight physiologic response cause muscles to tighten and to remain tight. Massage therapists, estheticians, and others who perform LDM often experience this combination of tissue conditions: chronic muscle stiffness and lymph stasis due to stress. This condition can be seen most clearly over thigh and hip muscles or shoulder and neck muscles.

Identifying the Causes of Ordinary Edema

Lacking Exercise

Exercise in which muscles alternately contract and relax stimulates lymph circulation in the muscle and cleanses muscle tissue. Muscle contraction and relaxation also affect nearby lymph vessels, stimulating them to contract. If the muscles stay contracted due to overexercise or flaccid due to lack of exercise, lymph circulation decreases drastically inside muscles and edema can result. This is particularly true as people age.

Dieting Poorly

The body maintains a specific salt-to-fluid ratio. The more salt a person consumes, the more water will be retained in the tissues to balance the salt. Water buildup contributes to edema. Americans commonly eat food high in sodium, so this type of edema is common and usually temporary. It responds to massage and improved diet, as well as added fluid intake.

Besides high sodium, foods like strawberries and avocados, which are common allergens, can cause swelling.

Sustaining Scar Tissue and Soft-Tissue Injury

When tissue is damaged, blood and lymph vessels rupture. Lymph circulation is inhibited by vessel damage. As the injured area heals and scar tissue forms, lymph circulation does not always improve. Lymph vessels and blood vessels grow in the new scar tissue, but they do not necessarily connect to the lymph vessels on the other side of the scar. Scar tissue can result from injury, surgery, or infection. Edema tends to form on the side of the scarring distal to, or farthest from, the nodes. Small pockets of edema can remain for years in an injury area. Even when many years elapse after an injury, and the accompanying edema has become chronic, the edema responds to a combination of connective tissue massage and LDM.

Suffering Heart or Kidney Disease

Heart and kidney diseases affect fluid circulation in the body. When the heart or kidneys are diseased, their ability to handle fluid is compromised. Fluid builds in the extremities, hands and arms, feet and legs. Lymph massage stimulates lymph circulation and returns fluid to the heart. As a result, blood volume increases, which, in the case of a person with heart disease, could overload an already weakened heart. Similarly, because the kidneys regulate blood volume, an increase in blood volume could overload already weakened kidneys.

Taking Medications

Various medications contribute to edema, particularly steroids like cortisone and hormone therapy. Chemotherapy for cancer can cause edema as a side effect.

Undergoing Radiation Therapy

Radiation therapy scars the tissue through which it passes, causing obstructive edema. Lymph vessels in the area are damaged along with other tissues, so lymph flow is obstructed in a large area.

Having Allergies

Insect bites and other allergens stimulate the inflammatory response that causes swelling. Because insects sometimes inject poisons with the bite or sting, massage should not be performed in the swelling area while symptoms are acute. Once symptoms subside and the area is no longer sensitive, massage is safe.

Experiencing the Menstrual Cycle

Water retention and/or a swollen abdomen and extremities are common before or during the menstrual cycle. Gentle lymph massage on the abdomen during menses is safe, but no deep massage should be performed.

Withstanding Emotional Tension

Stress is infrequently recognized as a cause of edema, yet practitioners commonly experience that chronic tension due to stress contributes to edema in the local area. For example, people suffering muscle-tension headaches often have palpable edema in the region of the occipital muscles due to spasm and inflammation in strained suboccipital muscles. With migraine headaches, elevated blood pressure in the cerebral arteries can produce edema in the tissues below the cranium.[24]

Describing Edema

Edema feels soft and spongy, though the skin may be tight. When edema is present, it is difficult to palpate such underlying structures as muscles and bones. Early stages of edema may have the pitting characteristic. To identify pitting, press a fingertip into the tissue, then withdraw it. Any remaining indentation is called pitting edema. The indentation may fill quickly or remain visible for a while. Tissue can be tender when compressed or painful because the swelling is pressing on nerves.

Stagnant tissue fluid (edema) contains proteins, microorganisms, and toxins. Microorganisms reproduce, causing infections. Protein buildup in tissues triggers inflammation. Because of the chronic edema that accompanies chronic inflammation, the tissue changes in texture and appearance, becoming thicker, less flexible, reddened, and coarse.

Edema is abnormal, so its presence indicates pathology of some sort, from temporary conditions caused by inactivity or minor injury to serious illnesses such as heart or kidney disease. Edema that does not abate in a day or two should be evaluated by a physician to rule out serious health problems.

Edematous tissues have poor oxygenation, poor nutrition, poor waste removal, reduced function, and heal slowly after injury. Edema can become chronic, leading to chronic inflammation and fibrosis, making the edematous tissue coarser, thicker, less flexible, and more tender due to increased neurofibrils in the injury area.[25, 26] In the most serious cases, edema becomes lymphedema.

Review Questions

1. How does dietary salt intake contribute to edema?

2. What are the common causes of obstructive edema?

3. How does exercise affect lymph circulation in muscles?

4. Besides obstruction, what other factors may contribute to edema?

5. Describe pitting edema.

6. What tissue changes occur with chronic edema?

CHAPTER 7

Lymph Drainage Massage: Indications and Contraindications

Lymph drainage massage is a valuable technique for many kinds of practitioners. While historically associated with the medical treatment of lymphedema, LDM has many applications for clients with less serious problems. It is used for cosmetic reasons, to improve the appearance and health of the skin, and to treat cellulite. While LDM is very gentle and safe, it stimulates physiological changes in the body and should not be used in some instances. Therapists should be familiar with LDM contraindications and should be prepared, when necessary, to speak with the client's physician before proceeding with the massage.

Working with Edema

While LDM was developed to treat edema and is very effective, it is important to know the cause of the edema before proceeding. Edema can sometimes be a symptom of serious conditions that can be aggravated by massage. Anyone who has chronic edema and does not know the cause should consult a physician to rule out serious health problems before receiving LDM.

Effecting Lymph Drainage Massage before and after Surgery

LDM may be used before and after surgery, including cosmetic surgery, to speed healing and reduce edema. Before surgery, LDM helps to remove stagnant fluid from tissues and increase blood flow, which brings nutrition to the tissues. LDM is also deeply relaxing, so it can lessen the client's stress and anxiety. Because the massage is so deeply relaxing, in fact somewhat hypnotic, the therapist can help clients by listening to their feelings about the surgery and by making positive statements about the outcome. One of the most beneficial effects of massage in a medical setting is that it meets the clients' needs for support and nurturing, needs that physicians and families cannot always provide.

After surgery, LDM can help to remove inflammation, speed healing, and reduce scar tissue. However, because of the risk of infection and the risk of blood clots, LDM should never be performed in connection with surgery without the approval, and possibly the direction, of the client's physician. It may be necessary to delay massage until the physician releases the client and the client needs no more medical treatment, at which time the client will have healed completely and massage is more likely to be safe.

Navigating Soft-Tissue Injury

In the case of soft-tissue injury, LDM speeds healing and reduces swelling. Do not massage immediately after an injury, however. All injuries, such as sports injuries, car accidents, falls, and so on, should be examined to rule out serious underlying conditions before massage. After appropriate medical treatment, and after such symptoms as pain and inflammation have decreased, LDM helps to speed healing, reduce inflammation and pain, and improve scars.

Treating a Sluggish Immune System

Frequent colds and allergies are indications for LDM. Basically healthy adults should be able to resist most mild illnesses to which they are exposed. If a client is frequently ill with minor illnesses and recovers slowly, the lymphatic system may be sluggish. In that case, LDM will stimulate the lymph circulation and potentially improve the condition. Encourage a client who is frequently ill with minor illnesses to have LDM regularly, daily if possible for a week, or at least once a week for three months.

Relieving Stress and Tension

Stress triggers the sympathetic nervous system, the well-known fight-or-flight state, arousing all the body's defenses. Chemicals like adrenaline are secreted into the bloodstream, causing muscles to tense. The heart and respiratory rates increase, organ function decreases, and the immune system is suppressed. Chronic stress results in chronic "racing" of the human system, with resulting stress on internal organs and functions and decreased disease resistance. In the long run, physical and mental reactions to stress can contribute to degenerative disease. Massage, and especially LDM, trigger the parasympathetic nervous system, which has the opposite effect on the body. Muscles relax, heart and breath rates decrease, and clients move into a drowsy state of relaxation that promotes healing and balance.

Addressing Chronic Fatigue, Mild Depression, and Chronic Soft-Tissue Pain

Symptoms like fatigue, mild depression, and chronic soft-tissue pain call for the gentleness of lymph massage. It is important for a person who has these symptoms and does not know the cause to have a physical examination by a physician, an acupuncturist, or another licensed health-care provider to rule out serious health problems. If there is no serious illness underlying the symptoms, LDM can be given with good results; it will stimulate the immune system and has an energizing effect on the body's *qi* or vital energy.

Working with Traveler's Edema

Enforced inactivity, such as sitting on an airplane for several hours, causes edema. Interstitial fluids respond to gravity, causing swelling in the feet, hands, and buttocks of a person who has to sit without moving very much for a few hours. LDM can remove edema and reduce the pain and stiffness that accompany it. However, there is risk of blood clots when someone has been sitting still for a long time. If clients have pain in the calf and the calf is red, hot, swollen, and painful, there may be a blood clot. Do *not* massage. Instead, refer the clients to their physicians immediately for diagnosis and treatment.

Achieving a Healthful Diet

An excess of salty food causes the body to retain water, resulting in edema. LDM can remove excess fluid from tissues, and return the fluid to the bloodstream for excretion through the kidneys. Encourage the client to drink more water and to reduce salt intake.

Mitigating Scar Tissue

Scar tissue blocks lymph flow. Lymph vessels damaged by injury or surgery do not necessarily grow together and connect through scar tissue. Tissue on the distal side of the scar tends to accumulate fluid. LDM reduces edema and also softens and minimizes scars, improving circulation. Massaging as soon as allowable after an injury or surgery actually helps scars to develop in a more organized way so that they become smaller, smoother, more flexible, and stronger.

Improving Cellulite

LDM is an important part of a cellulite-regulation program. Information on a program for regulating cellulite (lipedema) is given later in the text.

Enhancing the Skin

Unhealthy skin caused by poor circulation responds to LDM. The massage removes wastes and toxins from skin cells and improves lymph circulation so that the appearance of the skin is greatly enhanced. This is particularly useful in facial work. LDM helps such conditions as acne, rosacea, and excema. However, it is important to avoid massage during the acute phase of any skin condition.

LDM benefits the red, thickened, coarse skin that results from chronic edema and that is common in the lower extremities of clients with lymphedema and in clients who are obese.

Do not massage infected skin, including acne; areas that are burned, scraped, cut, or scratched; or areas that have any sort of abnormal drainage. Allow these areas to heal before massaging.

Lowering Blood Pressure

LDM lowers blood pressure temporarily, which benefits clients with high blood pressure. However, LDM should not be performed when elevated blood pressure coexists with congestive heart failure. Heart disease, such as congestive heart failure, is an LDM contraindication.

Take care with clients who have low blood pressure. LDM lowers blood pressure, so there is the danger that clients may become dizzy or faint upon standing after an LDM session. Avoid lengthy sessions and be sure clients are awake and feeling fine before standing. Sitting on the massage table with the legs dangling for a few minutes before standing reduces the risk of fainting.

Identifying Other Lymph Drainage Massage Contraindications

Although LDM is very beneficial to most people, some conditions contraindicate the massage. Some contraindications are absolute, some merely require that the therapist take precautions or consult with the client's physician before performing the massage.

Targeting Cancer

Traditionally, massage has been contraindicated for patients with active cancer for fear of causing the cancer to metastasize. However, there is no compelling evidence that LDM is dangerous for cancer patients. In fact, a client's physician may feel that the benefits from touch therapy outweigh the risks and thus recommend massage, including lymph massage.[27] However, the decision whether to give LDM to a person with active cancer should not be made independently. When clients are very ill and receiving treatment, the massage therapist should consult with the clients' health-care providers before giving the massage. This is especially true when clients are undergoing chemotherapy for the treatment of cancer. When a client is in remission and no longer being treated for cancer, LDM is generally considered safe.

Treating Open Wounds, Rashes, and Inflamed Skin Conditions

Any skin conditions that are contagious, infected, open or discharging fluid, or inflamed (red, hot, swollen, painful) are contraindicated for LDM or any kind of massage.

Lowering Fever and Infections

Fever, part of the body's natural healing processes, is a sign that a client is ill. This is an LDM contraindication. Encourage a client with a fever to rest and recover. When the fever is very high (over 103° F) or lasts for more than a few days, the client should see a physician or an acupuncturist, not a massage therapist or facialist. When an infection such as a cold or the flu could be transferred to the therapist or to the therapist's other clients, do not give lymph massage during the acute phase.

Inflammation (redness, swelling, heat, and pain) in any area of the body is a sign of injury, illness, or infection. Determine the cause of the inflammation before proceeding. In the case of chronic infections, massage may cause a flare-up of the infection, worsening the condition. Check with the client's physician before giving massage.

Working with Heart, Kidney, or Liver Disease

If major organs in the body, such as the heart, kidneys, or liver, are damaged and unable to function normally, edema may occur. However, even though edema is present, LDM is not appropriate. LDM, because it returns fluid to the cardiovascular system, increases blood volume. A weak heart may be unable to handle the increased load, stressing the heart. The kidneys control blood volume by excreting excess fluid. If the kidneys are failing, the increased volume of fluid in the blood can be too stressful. Give LDM to no one who has had a heart attack or heart surgery in the previous year, who has congestive heart failure or kidney failure, or who is undergoing kidney dialysis. When the client has liver disease, consult with the client's physician before giving massage.[28]

Improving Asthma

LDM may trigger an asthma attack in those with severe asthma. Do not give LDM during or following an asthma attack. If the client has a history of being hospitalized with asthma, or is on daily medication, give very short sessions until tolerance is determined.

Relieving Allergies

Allergic symptoms result from an overreaction of the immune system to allergens. Do not give LDM during an allergic reaction, as this stimulates lymph circulation and immune function and can spread histamines. After the client has recovered from acute allergic symptoms, it is safe to proceed with LDM. Regular LDM to the face and neck helps chronic sinus infections and allergies.

Understanding the Thyroid

It is possible to aggravate hyperthyroidism by massaging over the area of the thyroid. For clients with thyroid disease, any style of massage is contraindicated for the area of the thyroid, which is the front of the neck between the two sternocleidomastoid muscles.[29, 30]

Decreasing Blood Clots, Phlebitis, and Varicose Veins

Blood clots and phlebitis are contraindications for any kind of massage. Blood clots are possible during the first 2 weeks following surgery or injury, and massage can cause a blood clot to break loose and move through the circulatory system. Such an occurrence is potentially life threatening. It is best to avoid massage entirely for 2 weeks after surgery, unless the client's physician deems it safe.

If a client has a history of phlebitis or is taking blood-thinning medication, such as Coumadin (Warfarin), consult the physician before giving a massage. When in doubt, learn to perform Homan's test. Squeeze the calf. If severe pain results when the calf is released, refer the client to a physician immediately for phlebitis evaluation.

Closely examine varicose veins before massaging the area. If the area with varicose veins is warmer than surrounding tissue, reddened, swollen, and painful, do not give massage. An area with spider veins and protruding veins that are not red, hot, swollen, and painful may be massaged carefully. The very light pressure of LDM is safe as long as the veins are asymptomatic.

Undergoing Organ Transplants

Patients who have had organ transplants take immune-suppressing medication so that their bodies will not reject their transplanted organs. Therapists should not give immune-stimulating massage to any client who has had a major organ transplant without first consulting the client's physician.

Review Questions

1. Using the contraindications discussed in this chapter, create an intake form to use in your practice.

2. Using the indications discussed in this chapter, create a brochure that explains the benefits of LDM to your clients.

3. List the absolute LDM contraindications.

4. When should the therapist consult the client's physician before giving massage?

CHAPTER 8

Lymph Drainage Massage Principles

Because the European medical establishment prescribes and uses LDM, it is perhaps the most researched and scientifically validated form of massage in the world. A significant body of scientific evidence supports the effectiveness of massage in reducing edema.[31-35]

Beginning to Understand Lymph Drainage Massage

Probably the most famous style of LDM is the Dr. Vodder method. Emil and Estrid Vodder, while working and studying in France early in the twentieth century, intuitively developed a method of moving fluid through the lymphatic system using massage. The techniques the Vodders developed were based on their understanding of the physiology of the lymphatic system at that time. Although they demonstrated empirically the success of their technique, it was many years before science could validate the hypotheses they developed in their work. In the nearly 70 years since the Vodders introduced their new technique, many others have added to the body of knowledge about manual lymph drainage.

While very effective, the Vodder method is not the only useful method for moving lymph. I, for instance, observed tui na massage techniques reducing edema effectively while studying massage in the orthopedic department of Guang An Men Hospital, a teaching hospital in Beijing, China.

The massage techniques Drs. Vodder and others developed and advocated are often detailed and complicated, making it difficult to learn the techniques and limiting the public's access to the treatment. Most LDM techniques are labor intensive, complicated, time consuming, and expensive, because serious cases of lymphedema require daily therapy. However, modern evidence indicates that success depends on only a few necessary principles, and in fact simple self-treatment procedures can very effectively move lymph.[36]

Adhering to Lymph Drainage Massage Principles

When moving lymph fluid, certain principles are more meaningful than specific hand movements. While teaching and practicing LDM over some years I developed the following important principles. The greatest success in reducing edema and stimulating lymph circulation results when these principles are followed. Massage techniques that do not conform to these principles do not move lymph as efficiently but they may still be beneficial.

Move the Skin

There is a rich bed of lymph capillaries in the superficial tissues, close to the surface of the skin, in the outer layers of the skin, and edema occurs in these superficial tissues more often than in deep tissue. LDM focuses on this bed of lymph capillaries. Success depends on moving the skin. Stretching the skin lengthwise, horizontally, and diagonally stretches the initial lymphatics and lymph capillaries, stimulating them to contract.[37] Moving the skin also pulls the microfilaments that connect the initial lymphatics to the surrounding tissues, causing the endothelial flaps to open and allowing interstitial fluid to enter the initial lymphatics.

Apply Gentle Pressure

The softer the tissue, or the more severe the edema, the lighter the pressure of the massage must be. Vodder estimated the proper pressure for lymph drainage to be less than 30 torr, or 8 ounces per square inch.[38, 39] This figure is very close to the pressures Zweifach and Prather found collecting lymphatics in 1975. The pressure in the peripheral lymphatics is even less, approximately less than 1 to 8 ounces per square inch.[40]

The recommended pressure for effectively moving lymph and reducing edema is between $\frac{1}{2}$ ounce and 8 ounces of pressure per square inch. At the beginning of the massage, the pressure should be closer to $\frac{1}{2}$ or 1 ounce per square inch. As the massage progresses and the therapist feels tissue change, the pressure can increase, becoming closer to 8 ounces per square inch. To be more accurate, it helps to practice by stroking the surface of a postage scale until one can easily keep the pressure in the recommended range.

Effect Slow Movements

The greater the inertial mass (the amount of fluid in the tissue to be moved), the slower the movements must be. When there is a great deal of fluid to be moved, massage strokes may be repeated as slowly as six circles per minute, approximately the rate at which the peripheral lymphatics contract.[41] The rate of lymph flow is relatively slow compared to blood flow, and lymph flow is variable, depending on outside influences. Therefore, LDM must be correspondingly slow, synchronizing with physiologic processes. As the therapist begins to feel tissue change, the movements can be relatively faster.

Move in the Proper Direction

Move lymph toward the lymph nodes in the neck, axilla, and groin. The lymph vessels effectively divide the body into four sections, excluding the head. Each section consists of a limb and the adjacent quadrant of the trunk. The four quadrants are the:

1. right arm and upper-right quadrant of the trunk.
2. left arm and upper-left quadrant of the trunk.
3. right leg and lower-right quadrant of the trunk.
4. left leg and lower-left quadrant of the trunk.

The basic pattern of massage is to drain lymph nodes first, then the related quadrant of the trunk, and gradually work outward to the end of the extremity. The purpose of massaging the lymph nodes first is to make room for more fluid, which will be drained from the adjacent areas. Lymph circulation slows at the lymph nodes, as discussed in the chapter on lymph circulation, and when the therapist starts massaging at the extremity of the limb and works toward the lymph nodes, the fluid tends to accumulate in the tissues surrounding the lymph nodes, causing swelling and discomfort.

Achieve the Right Rhythm and Repetition

Smooth, rhythmic movements are essential to massage's success. One effect of LDM may be that it coordinates the contractions of the lymphatics, which can be erratic. Slow, rhythmic repetition of massage movements stimulates a wave in the lymph fluid, similar to intestinal peristalsis.[42] Once therapists are in contact with the skin, they should maintain connection with the same area for at least a minute, repeating the stroke with the same pressure, direction, and speed until there is a palpable change in the tissue. Begin with six to ten repetitions of the massage stroke in a minute, increasing the minutes on an area if the tissue does not respond.

Identifying Lymph Drainage Patterns

Understanding the direction in which lymph drains is vital for the success of LDM. The basic pattern of LDM follows the direction of lymph flow from the extremities and watersheds to the cervical, axillary, and inguinal nodes (Figure 8–1a). The lymph vessels resemble four large branching trees made up of lymph capillaries and vessels. The lymph vessels drain

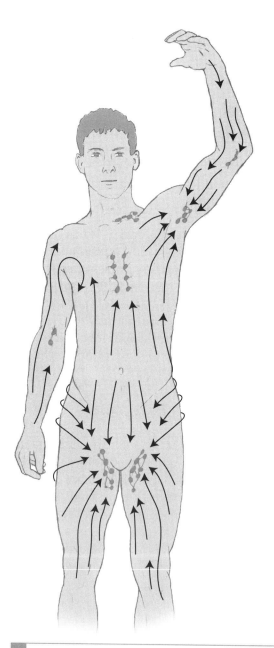

Figure 8–1a Direction of lymph drainage, anterior.

fluid from the outermost reaches of the trees (the watersheds and the extremities) toward the axillary and inguinal nodes (tree trunks) and, from the nodes, lymph vessels leading to the interior body are like the roots. At the watersheds, the branches of the trees overlap, but the drainage pattern is clearly demarcated (Figure 8–1b).

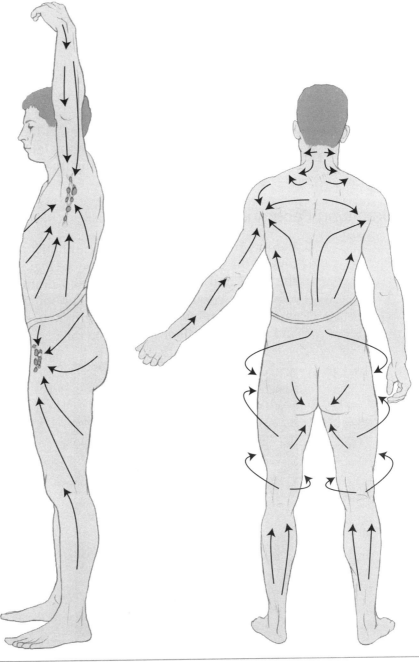

Figure 8–16 Direction of lymph drainage, lateral and posterior.

Working in the Upper Body

In the upper body, between the waist and the clavicle, the superficial lymphatics drain to the axillary lymph nodes. The right arm and right side of the trunk drain toward the right axillary nodes. The left arm and the left side of the trunk drain toward the left axillary nodes. However, the superficial lymphatics over the sternum drain upward to the neck, rather than toward the axillary nodes (Figure 8–2).

Moving through the Lower Body

In the lower body, superficial lymphatics drain to the inguinal nodes (Figure 8–3). The lymphatic vessels take the shortest route, so the superficial lymphatics in the buttocks drain laterally around the body to the inguinal nodes in front. The lymphatics in the posterior thigh divide; the lateral area of the thigh drains laterally around the leg, and the medial area of the thigh drains medially around the leg to the inguinal nodes. Lymph from the right leg and right lower quadrant of the trunk drains into the right inguinal nodes. Lymph from the left leg and the left lower quadrant of the trunk drains into the left inguinal nodes.

Executing Face and Neck Patterns

Lymph from the superficial lymphatics of the head drains inferiorly toward the lymph nodes in the neck (Figure 8–4). Lymph from the top of the head and the back of the head drains to the occipital nodes, then toward the cervical nodes in the general area of the sternocleidomastoid muscle. Lymph from the facial lymphatics drains toward the preauricular and mandibular nodes, then into the cervical nodes.

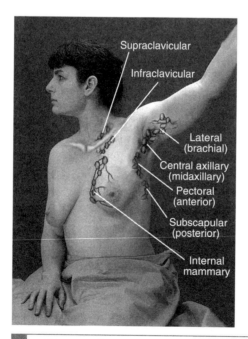

Figure 8–2 Lymph nodes of the upper quadrant.

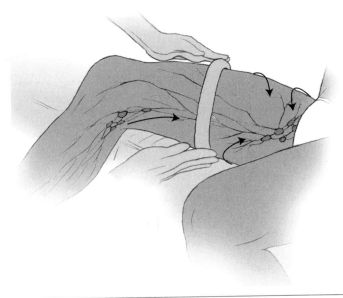

Figure 8-3 Location of nodes of the lower quadrant.

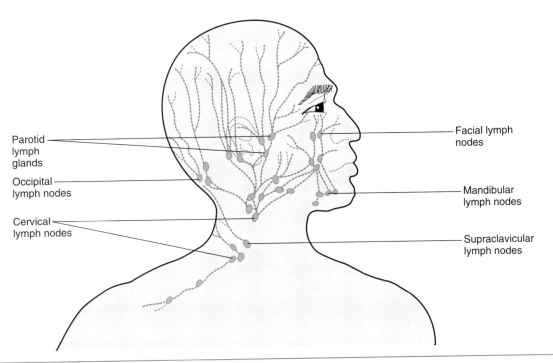

Parotid lymph glands

Occipital lymph nodes

Cervical lymph nodes

Facial lymph nodes

Mandibular lymph nodes

Supraclavicular lymph nodes

Figure 8-4 Lymph nodes of the face and neck.

Identifying Watersheds

The direction of lymph drainage in the four trunk quadrants is not exact. Lymph capillaries form a network over the whole body, and the drainage of lymph in the four trunk quadrants is interconnected (Figure 8–5). In each area, most of the lymphatics drain toward the nearest nodes. However, some lymph capillaries, especially along the margins of the quadrants of the trunk, drain to the opposite side. Around the waist, for instance, some lymph capillaries drain upward to the axillary nodes, and others drain downward to the inguinal nodes.

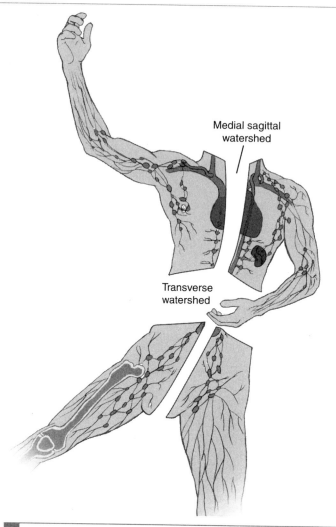

Figure 8–5 Medial sagittal and transverse watersheds.

Because of this, interstitial fluid that accumulates in areas blocked by obstructions like scar tissue or removal of nodes may be directed to nodes on the opposite side of the body, bypassing the obstruction. So, for instance, while most of the lymph vessels in the upper-right quadrant of the trunk drain into the right axillary nodes, some are connected to the vessels of the left-upper trunk and the right-lower trunk. When there is an obstruction, such as scar tissue or removal of lymph nodes in one quadrant, the edema resulting in that quadrant affects adjacent quadrants of the trunk. The edema can be routed to the adjacent trunk quadrants through massage, making it possible to move lymph around obstructions, into the lymph nodes.[43]

Executing Basic Massage Procedure

Begin by draining the lymph nodes of the affected quadrant. Because lymph drainage slows at the lymph nodes, the nodes must be drained first to make room for fluid drained from surrounding areas. Then, massage adjacent areas, moving fluid in the tissues near the lymph nodes into the lymph nodes themselves. Massage the related trunk quadrant, working lymph fluid toward the nodes.

Next, massage the affected limb proximal to distal, which means gradually working from the areas adjacent to the nodes out toward the distal end of the extremity. For example, if the ankle were swollen, the therapist would empty the inguinal nodes on the same side of the body as the swollen ankle first. Next, she would massage the lower abdomen and buttocks on the same side as the affected ankle. Then she would massage the thigh (beginning close to the inguinal lymph nodes), the knee, and the lower limb (beginning at the knee and moving toward the ankle), gradually emptying the lymphatic vessels in the areas between the inguinal nodes and the edema. Finally, the therapist would massage the edematous ankle area itself, then work back up to the lymph nodes, emptying the inguinal nodes again at the end of the session. Depending on the degree of edema, the therapist may need to repeat the procedure until she feels a definite change in the edematous tissue.

For obstructive edema, a chronic swelling due to scar tissue from surgery, injury, or radiation, the general procedure is to massage the well side first, then the obstructed side. Following are the basic steps:

1. Massage the lymph nodes on the affected and unaffected sides of the body, inguinal nodes for lower body edema, and axillary and cervical nodes for upper body edema.

2. Massage the trunk quadrant on the well side first. For instance, if the left arm is edematous due to scar tissue or the removal of axillary nodes, perform LDM on the right-upper quadrant of the trunk first.

3. Massage the trunk quadrant on the edematous side. In our example of the edematous left arm, this would be the upper-left quadrant of the trunk, closest to the area of lymph stasis.

4. Massage the anterior and posterior of the shoulder and chest regions.

5. Massage the proximal area of the edematous limb. In this case, that would be the upper-left arm, beginning at the shoulder, moving toward the elbow.

6. Massage the distal area of the edematous limb. In this case, that would be the lower-left arm, from the elbow toward the hand.

If the work has been performed carefully and slowly, by the time the therapist massages the entire extremity, the lymph should be moving more freely, and the lymphatic vessels should be contracting rhythmically. The therapist would then massage back toward the lymph nodes from the hand, moving with relatively more pressure and speed. The therapist would finish by massaging the lymph nodes again, then follow with closing strokes of the therapist's choosing, such as effleurage.

Completing Basic Lymph Drainage Massage Movements

A wide variety of movements are taught in LDM. As long as therapists follow basic principles, any movement, whether circular, J-shaped, semi-circular, or other, will work. There is no substitute for demonstration by an instructor.

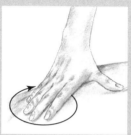
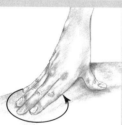

Using the Stationary Circle

The basis of all LDM is the **stationary circle**. The stationary circle has two important components: (1) a slight compression at the beginning of the movement and (2) a stretch of the tissues at the end of the movement. This move is called the stationary circle because it is important to remain stationary and repeat the movement six to ten times before moving to adjacent areas.

Using flat fingers, gently contact the skin, compress slightly, and stretch the tissue in a circular movement, clockwise or counterclockwise. Lymphatic capillaries are very close to the surface of the skin, so there is no need for deep pressure. The circular movement will stretch the lymph capillaries in different directions, stimulating them to contract. Also, gentle stationary circles cause the initial lymphatics to open, allowing interstitial fluid to enter through the endothelial flaps.

Doing the Pump

The pump is used on the extremities. Place the thumb on one side of the limb and wrap the palm and flat fingers around to the opposite side. Then, gently compress and stretch the skin with a scooping motion toward the appropriate lymph nodes, releasing pressure at the end of the movement. Repeat the pump movement until there is a palpable change in the skin.

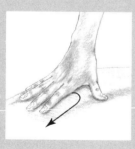

Using "J" Strokes

To use the "J" stroke, using the flat hand gently compress the skin. Twist and push toward the lymph nodes. This stroke is very useful on the back of the torso and on the thighs, front and back.

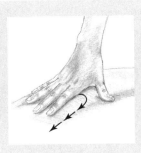

Taking the Jay Walk

To take the Jay walk, using the "J" stroke move purposefully (march) toward the nodes in a direct line. When performing the Jay walk, rather than repeating the "J" stroke in one area, the therapist moves the hand closer to the nodes with each repetition. This is more useful at the end of the massage, when working back toward the nodes from the distal end of the arm or leg.

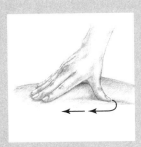

Effecting the Thumb Walk

To effect the thumb walk, use the thumbs to make the "J" strokes. This technique is useful in small areas like the face, around bony protuberances, and on the hands or feet. The thumbs are stronger than the fingers, so be sure not to exert excessive pressure when performing this movement.

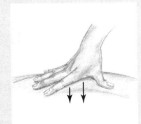

Doing the Flat Hand Push

In the flat hand push, use the flat palmar surface of the entire hand to first gently compress the skin, then stretch it toward the nodes. Repeat with one or both hands until there is a palpable change in the tissue. This stroke mechanically moves fluid, sweeping it through the lymphatics, but, because it only stretches the lymphatics in one direction, it is not as effective as movements that stretch the skin in a semicircle. It is, however, a useful stroke for self-massage.

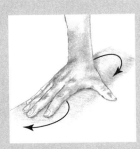

Completing the Figure 8

To complete the figure 8, using the flat surface of the whole hand compress the skin slightly, and stretch it in a figure eight movement. The flat fingers move counterclockwise, and the palm, as it follows the fingers, moves clockwise. Imagine using the whole hand to trace a figure eight on the skin, or contact the skin with just the fingers and push the skin gently in a figure eight.

Gathering Additional Lymph Drainage Massage Information

- To save time, use two hands together to cover larger areas. Even though using two hands together saves time, the movements must still adhere to basic LDM principles: gentle, slow, rhythmic strokes that move the skin.

■ It helps to visualize the movement of lymph. Imagine hundreds of small streams converging to form a river that flows to the sea. LDM removes tiny blockages in the streams so that the fluid can flow freely toward its destination. Imagine that the work is smoothing the streambeds, coaxing rocks and other debris out of the way, and straightening the twists and bends to make the stream flow more easily.

■ Although therapists' hands do the work, it is important for the therapists to keep their body weight centered over the feet and to move from the *hara* or body center. Therapists should move their bodies with the massage strokes. This slows the work and makes the pace more even. The client feels more grounded. When therapists stand with most of the body weight on one foot or lean and stretch, the clients can feel the difference in the massage work.

■ When working for a long time on one area of the body, it is often better to sit in a chair rather than stand. The therapist should pull the chair very close to the massage table, sit well back in the chair with the weight centered on the buttocks, and support the spine with the back of the chair. Therapists can still move their bodies with the massage strokes, moving from the hips. Keep both feet planted on the floor.

■ Pay close attention to subtle changes in the tissue temperature, texture, and elasticity. As the work progresses, the skin should feel warmer, softer, looser, and more liquid.

■ Pay attention to the client's experience of the massage. Clients report such experiences as prickling sensations along the lymph pathways, heaviness, warmth, the need to urinate, and respiratory congestion during and after LDM. Skin that had been puffy or distended will begin to wrinkle slightly as the lymph fluid is drained from the area.

■ LDM requires discipline and concentration. Before beginning the massage, the therapist should take a few moments to center and focus on the work to be done. The ability to focus on the work despite distractions is key to success. Therapists who are distracted or daydream while giving massage will miss important, subtle changes in the tissue. With practice, and with discipline, therapists learn to sense the movement of lymph through tissues. Palpation skills become refined, and therapists move to new skill levels. This high level of sensitivity is worth the effort it takes to remain focused while doing repetitive work.

■ At the beginning of the massage the massage therapist or facialist should take a few moments to perform the following steps:

1. Check personal posture. The massage is more effective and feels better to clients when therapists have their weight centered on both feet, spine erect, head lifted, and chest expanded for easy breathing.

2. Concentrate on breathing slowly and regularly. Take a few slow breaths, inhaling through the nose and exhaling through the mouth with a slight pause at the end of each inhalation and exhalation.

3. Pay attention to the client's breathing. Is it regular or irregular, coming from the abdomen or chest, deep or shallow, fast or slow? When placing hands on the client's skin, take a moment to assess tissue condition. Is it cool or warm, pale or red, taut or flaccid? What is the extent and location of the edema, if any? Are there scars or other markings? Are there differences in the temperature of the skin in different areas? Are some areas more rigid than others?

4. During the massage, if distracted, repeat the preceding steps to regain focus. Pay attention to how the tissue changes during the session and how the client responds. With practice and focus it is possible to feel the movement of lymph through tissues. Because LDM is slow and repetitious, staying focused demands discipline on the part of the therapist. Discipline might be difficult at first, but it pays off in increased ability to palpate subtle changes in the movement of tissue fluid.

Review Questions

1. Who was the originator of modern LDM?

2. What is the purpose of moving the skin when applying LDM?

3. What is the optimal pressure for LDM?

4. Why is it important to repeat massage strokes when performing LDM and what is the recommended rate?

5. In what direction is the therapist trying to move the lymph when performing LDM?
   a. Toward the heart
   b. Toward the extremities
   c. Toward the lymph nodes

6. What is the basic pattern or order of movements in LDM?

7. What can happen if lymph nodes are not massaged first and last?

8. Why is slow, rhythmic repetition of strokes so important?
   a. To coordinate lymphatic contractions
   b. To stimulate a wave in lymph fluid
   c. To allow lymph to move at its own pace
   d. All of the above

9. From memory, draw a sketch of the pattern of lymph drainage to the trunk and extremities. Include the watersheds and the location of lymph nodes.

10. What are watersheds?

11. Because of the watersheds, lymph can be directed around obstructions and drained toward the nodes of the unaffected side of the body.
    a. True
    b. False

12. Why is the well or unaffected side massaged first when working with obstructive edema?

13. What is the basic movement or stroke in LDM and when should it be performed?

14. Why is the ability to focus and concentrate important in LDM? How can one increase the ability to concentrate?

The Lymph Drainage Massage Session

*A*s every experienced therapist knows, there is more to massage than just body work. One of the most important factors in successful massage is communication. The therapist may have to coax the client to communicate not only factual information about health history and the client's background, but less clear-cut information about the client's assumptions and expectations regarding the massage and its outcome. The more the therapist learns from the client, the more successful the massage.

Communicating Clearly and Fully

Massage therapists must also clearly communicate their purpose for the massage, the kind of massage and its effects, what will happen during the session, the therapists' expectations about client participation in the session, and expectations for the outcome of the massage. Also, therapists must communicate boundaries, policies, and procedures. This is time consuming, so therapists should allow time for adequate communication, especially before and after the first LDM session.

The client may want some information about the therapist's background, education, and experience with LDM. A brochure or flyer with this information is useful. Therapists should also ask clients why they are having

LDM, and what they expect the massage to achieve. Spend time educating the client, as there are many misconceptions about the purpose and effect of LDM.

Intake forms can save time and cover a lot of ground, so it is a good plan to have one ready for each new client. Allow clients to tell as much as they want about their health. People with chronic health problems may need to talk, and the information they provide is invaluable. When using intake forms, specifically ask about contraindications, and ask if there is anything additional the client thinks the therapist should know.

Explain procedures such as where the client will undress, where the massage will take place, where to hang clothes, and how to get on the massage table. Give the client control of the session: explain that the client has the right to ask questions, request changes, and tell the therapist if he or she is cold, uncomfortable, too warm, thirsty, or requires the bathroom.

Explain briefly how the massage will progress. Be sure to show the client where the lymph nodes are located, and explain why it is necessary to work in those areas. Because superficial lymph nodes are near private areas of the body, therapists should explain where they will put their hands and why. Doing so helps keep clients calm.

A wall chart that shows the locations of lymph nodes and the direction of lymph drainage helps illustrate LDM. Do not assume that clients know this type of information. Most people lack accurate information about the lymphatic system.

Beginning the Session

Use a gentle, slow effleurage to desensitize the skin against tickling. While performing effleurage, assess the condition of the tissue to be aware of changes occurring during the session. After the first few minutes of the session, when the client is visibly relaxing and demonstrating trust, encourage the client to rest quietly for a while. Some clients enjoy conversing with the therapist, but the therapist should remain focused on subtle changes in the tissue that indicate lymph movement.

Let the client know it is all right to ask questions about the work and to discuss anything else significant that may have been omitted from the intake interview, but subtly discourage chatter. Also, remind the client that it is all right to move the head, arms, or legs to be more comfortable and that it is all right to sigh, moan, snore, or make any other noise while relaxing.

Finishing the Session

Finish with gradually firmer effleurage to signify the end of the massage and the change from lymph work to the process of waking up. Use percussion or other stimulating techniques to ensure the client is awake enough to drive safely.

If the client has been lying still for a half hour or more, stretch the client's lower back to prevent a cramp on arising. Ask the client to turn onto the side and to pull the knees to the chest for a few minutes, or ask the client to turn over and then massage the lower back. Help the client sit and then stand. Allowing the client to sit on the massage table with the feet dangling for a few minutes will raise the client's blood pressure, preventing fainting. Make sure the client is oriented to time and place and is not dizzy. Instruct the client in follow-up (e.g., exercises, other sessions, referrals to other practitioners). Be sure to offer a drink of water after the massage.

After the session, record any additional information the client revealed about health history, the therapist's observations about the session results, anything the client says about the session results, and any recommendations made by the therapist.

Recording Client Information

Client records serve several purposes. A good intake form can help gather information about the client's health history and activity level, gives the therapist guidelines for discussing client's massage expectations, and suggest areas of concern so that the therapist can ask more questions and make better, more informed decisions. Also, a good intake form documents that the therapist observed the contraindications and referred the client to medical practitioners when appropriate.

Therapists should record each service or massage given to a client. Record observations, the client's report, the service/massage given to the client, and the outcomes and recommendations made to the client.

Occasionally, therapists are employed in facilities, like spas and resorts, that do not use intake forms. In these cases, therapists should discuss using intake forms with facility directors. When employers are unwilling to use intake forms, the therapist is responsible for asking each client for health information. Not doing so is malpractice.

Clients' records should include the following information:

- Personal Information

  Name

  Address

  Phone number

  Physician's name and number

  Emergency contact

  Reason for requesting LDM

- Health History

  Diagnosis, where applicable

  Date of injury, when applicable

  Recent medical, chiropractic, or acupuncture treatment

  Medications and their purposes

- Specifically ask about the following conditions:

  Heart (heart disease, heart surgery or heart attack in the past year, arrhythmia, congestive heart failure, pacemaker, taking Coumadin [Warfarin])

  Blood pressure (high or low)

  Blood clot (history, current condition, medications, permission from physician for massage)

  Phlebitis, varicose veins

  Liver disease or kidney disease

  Organ transplant

  Cancer (active or in remission, treatment such as chemotherapy or radiation, original cancer or metastasis)

  Injury, date of injury, treatment, level of pain, and disability

  Surgery, date of surgery, kind of surgery, outcome, follow-up, pain level

  Asthma

  Diabetes

  Pregnancy

  Allergies

  Edema (how it developed, how long it has existed, pain quality and severity, location, past treatment and outcome, does the physician recommend massage)

  Infection or illness

■ Record of Session

Changes in client's health since the original session

Client's report and expectations of massage (type of massage; areas of focus; location, level, and quality of pain; outcome of last session)

Therapist's observations

Type of treatment or massage given client

Session outcome

Recommendations

If a client objects to completing a health history, explain that all kinds of massage, including LDM, cause physiologic changes in the body and that massage can adversely affect some conditions. The therapist has a right and responsibility to request the information, and a client who is not willing to share the information is a poor risk.

Clients may be concerned about confidentiality. Any business that collects health information is legally obliged to protect that information. Such information should be kept in a locked file accessible only to those who need to know the information. Therapists should never discuss a client's health information where it can be overheard by anyone other than the therapist and client. Client information should never be released to any third party without the client's written consent or a court order.

Face and Neck Treatment Sequence

*U*nless there is edema and/or scar tissue elsewhere in the body that need attention, it is far more useful to give lymph drainage massage to the face and neck. The head and neck are rich with lymph nodes, because disease-causing organisms easily enter the body via the mouth, nose, and eyes. LDM stimulates the circulation of lymph and lymphocytes through the facial and cervical lymph nodes.

Identifying Face and Neck Indications and Contraindications

LDM to the face and neck very effectively reduces bruising and swelling following injury or surgery, including dental and cosmetic surgery. Because blood clots are a concern after surgery, LDM should not be offered until the client is released by the physician and requires no follow-up visits. Some physicians recommend LDM during healing. In that case, LDM should be performed according to the physician's instructions.

A physician should examine head and neck injuries to rule out serious conditions before massage is permissible. Open wounds, incisions, scratches, and abrasions should be allowed to heal before massage is offered.

Facial edema can be due to allergies, hormones, medication, fatigue, illness, infection, injury, excess salt in the diet, weeping, and so on. Because some of these conditions are contraindications, it is important to know the reason for the edema before proceeding. If the client is unsure and the edema persists, a medical examination may be in order before offering LDM. Once a proper diagnosis has been obtained and contraindications are ruled out, LDM may be used to reduce facial swelling.

LDM stimulates a sluggish immune system to more activity by increasing the circulation of lymph and lymphocytes. Encourage clients who are frequently ill with minor colds and similar illnesses to have a series of LDM sessions at the beginning of cold and flu season. Recommend at least three sessions in 1 week, although up to seven sessions in 1 week would be more beneficial.

Similarly, LDM benefits clients with low energy. Low energy can result from stress, overwork, illness, or depression, any of which can depress the immune system. Stimulating immune circulation will help a fatigued client resist illness. In contrast, clients with high energy levels who overwork and overexercise are prone to illness and injuries because they do not rest. LDM is deeply relaxing and may be used to help speed healing, as well as give overworked clients some rest.

Sometimes, clients who are fatigued believe they need deep massage work to feel better. Deep massage, or very firm pressure, can be exhausting and may require a few days of recovery time. Deep-tissue massage has its place, but it is inappropriate for conditions of fatigue. It may take some time to teach the client that deep work can be draining and that subtle work is highly effective and will increase his or her energy level.

Although LDM is focused on superficial tissues, the muscles underneath also respond to the light, skillfully directed touch and will relax. Pain due to muscle tension will reduce or disappear. For instance, LDM can help relax the muscles that cause muscle-tension headaches. When facial muscles relax, the facial expression softens and relaxes, which contributes to a more youthful and healthy look.

LDM carries toxins (microscopic organisms, foreign particles, the by-products of cellular energy combustion) away from the dermal tissues and allows increased nutrition to flow into the skin, improving the skin's condition. Regular LDM changes the complexion, causing the skin to glow with increased health. If, however, the skin is infected, or if there is acne that is red and inflamed, it is better to wait until the infection has cleared before proceeding with any kind of face massage.

Inflammation from injuries like whiplash causes edema as blood flow to the area increases, bringing a cleanup crew of cells that remove damaged tissue and rebuild. Also, muscles splint after an injury to protect the injured area from moving, making it more difficult for fluid to move out of the area. Clients will complain of stiff, swollen, painful necks with limited flexibility. LDM stimulates lymph circulation, removing excess fluid from the area and helping the injury to heal faster. It also relaxes muscles, making them more flexible and improving the range of motion.

If there is a serious injury, it is being splinted and supported by the contracted muscles and the swelling. Relaxing those muscles and reducing edema with massage can make things worse if there is a serious underlying injury, so massage is contraindicated until the injury has been examined to rule out fracture, torn ligaments, and so on. Once the acute symptoms have subsided, LDM is indicated to reduce swelling and speed healing. Once the injury has healed to the point that scar tissue has been deposited, LDM can be combined with connective tissue massage, such as deep-tissue massage or myofascial release. It helps reduce edema, it makes scar tissue softer and more flexible, and it helps contracted muscles relax. For more information, see the section on injuries later in the text.

Symptoms like stiffness, pain, limited movement, and muscle-tension headaches resulting from whiplash injuries can remain for years if the injury is treated ineffectively. LDM and connective-tissue massage can improve matters even years after injury.

Treating Chronically Swollen Lymph Nodes

Many people have chronically swollen lymph nodes, often from repeated infections and childhood illnesses. First, it is important to have the nodes examined to rule out more serious conditions. If no serious condition is causing the swollen nodes and no infection is present, regular LDM can help to reduce the size of the nodes and improve lymph circulation in the area. In this case, it is a good idea to teach the client to perform self-massage daily. Daily massage produces results faster.

A client who has had repeated infections and illnesses is sometimes prone to a healing crisis when receiving LDM. This means simply that the client might experience a flare-up of old symptoms. A healing crisis is not serious, but it can be alarming if the therapist or esthetician has not told the client about the possibility. Therapists and estheticians should familiarize themselves with the material later in this text on the subject of the healing crisis.

Heeding Precautions

Hands must be very clean before touching the face. Be sure to scrub under and around fingernails. Keep lotion or oil or aromatherapy oil out of the client's eyes. If using lotions, creams, or oils, consider placing a cotton pad over each eye. Use a warm, moist towel to clean the client's face before proceeding with the session. The towel has the added effect of relaxing muscles and stimulating lymph flow.

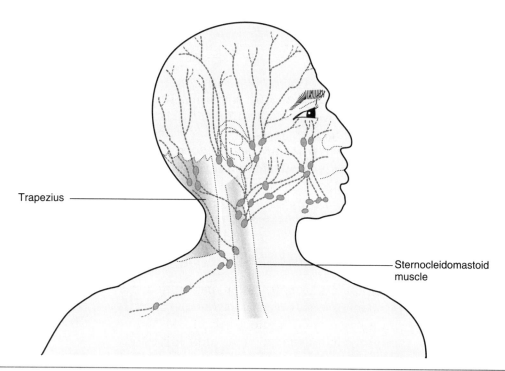

Trapezius

Sternocleidomastoid muscle

Figure 10–1 Locations of the trapezius and sternocleidomastoid muscles.

Locating Lymph Nodes on the Face and Neck

On the neck, lymph nodes are located in two triangles, one on each side of the neck, bound by the sternocleidomastoid muscle, the clavicle, and the superior border of the trapezius muscle (Figure 10–1). The apex of each triangle is on the neck immediately below the earlobe. Additional lymph nodes are below the mandible from the angle of the jaw to the chin and in the back behind the ears and along the base of the skull. On the face, nodes are in front of the ears, on the angle of the jaw anterior to the masseter muscle, and occasionally near the eyes, nose, and mouth.

Observing and Palpating Lymph Nodes on the Face and Neck

Before proceeding, and while the client is seated and facing the therapist, look carefully at the client's face and neck. Look for asymmetry and any swelling or signs of inflammation in front of or behind the ears, under the eyes, along the jaw line, in the neck, and in the supraclavicular triangle. In a healthy person, the lymph nodes should not be visibly swollen or inflamed. When swelling or inflammation is present, discuss the condition with the client before proceeding. If the client does not know the reason for the swelling or inflammation and has never had it examined, do *not* proceed with the massage until a physician has ruled out serious health conditions. Swollen lymph nodes indicate infection, which is a contraindication for massage. For instance, swollen lymph nodes under the jaw line can indicate a dental infection, swollen tonsils can indicate a sinus infection, and swollen nodes near the ear can indicate an ear infection. Swollen nodes can also indicate a more serious health problem, such as cancer, so they should definitely be examined.

Some clients will have chronically enlarged lymph nodes due to a serious underlying health problem or to such chronic infections as sinusitis or tonsillitis. Lymph nodes can also be scarred by repeated infections and remain enlarged after the infection has disappeared.

Upon observing the lymph nodes, the next step is to palpate the lymph nodes. When the client is lying supine on the massage table, palpate the lymph nodes of the face and neck. Using medium to light pressure, massage in small circles over the areas where the lymph nodes are located, attempting to locate small, pea-sized masses that can be moved. Use Figure 10–2 as a guide for locating lymph nodes. Palpate the tissues behind and in front of the ears (post- and preauricular nodes), under the jaw line from the chin (submental nodes) to the angle of the jaw (submandibular nodes), along the sternocleidomastoid muscle (anterior cervical chain) and the superior edge of the trapezius muscle (posterior cervical chain), and in the supraclavicular triangle.

In a healthy person, lymph nodes are generally quite small and cannot be palpated. If nodes are palpable, discuss this with the client before proceeding

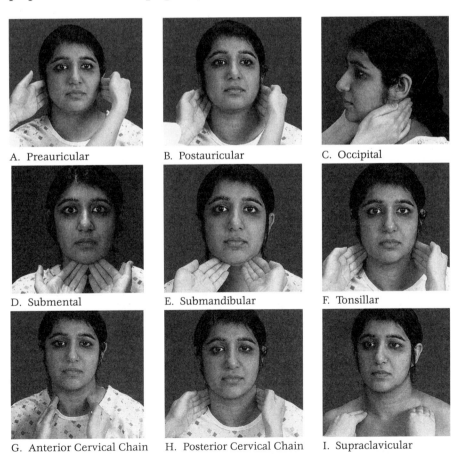

A. Preauricular   B. Postauricular   C. Occipital

D. Submental   E. Submandibular   F. Tonsillar

G. Anterior Cervical Chain   H. Posterior Cervical Chain   I. Supraclavicular

Figure 10–2 Palpation of cervical nodes.

with the massage. Find out how long the nodes have been enlarged, whether the client is aware of any infection, whether the nodes are tender, and whether the client has seen a physician about the enlarged nodes. If the client does not know the history of the problem and has not seen a physician, do *not* proceed with the massage. Before massage, refer the client to a physician for examination to rule out serious underlying health conditions.

Establishing a Lymph Drainage Pattern on the Face and Neck

Lymph drainage on the face is usually divided into two areas by drawing lines from the apex of the nose to the angle of the jaw on either side, creating a triangle. Inside the triangle, including the nose, mouth, chin, and jawline, lymph drains to the nodes under the mandible, then down through the anterior chain of nodes in the neck toward the lymphatic ducts at the medial ends of the clavicle (Figure 10–3).

Outside the triangle, including the forehead, temple, and cheeks, lymph drains to the preauricular nodes and the deep nodes on the neck below the earlobe, before draining through the nodes in the neck toward the lymphatic ducts located near the medial ends of the clavicle.

Lymphatic vessels of the scalp drain posteriorly through the occipital nodes, then through cervical nodes. Lymph vessels on the back of the neck drain anteriorly toward the cervical nodes.

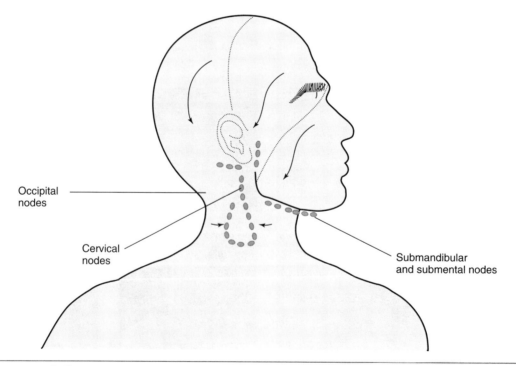

Occipital nodes

Cervical nodes

Submandibular and submental nodes

Figure 10–3 Direction of lymph drainage on the face and neck.

The basic pattern for the massage is to empty the lymph nodes on the neck, then to massage the entire neck before massaging the face. On the face, empty the lymph nodes first, then drain the lymph vessels on the face and scalp, draining the inner triangle first, then the remainder of the face and the scalp. Finish by draining the nodes on the neck again.

Supplies

- Very small bolster or rolled towel under the client's neck; bolster under the knees, if requested; warm covering during the massage session
- Warm, moist towel to relax the facial muscles, encourage lymph flow, and remove any surface particles before the massage begins
- Lotion or cream for lubrication

Optional

- Aromatherapy oils
- Eye pads

Extending Lymph Drainage Massage to the Face and Neck

Face and neck LDM is a nice add-on service to offer a client who is having a body wrap, but the therapist must be sure the client does not become dehydrated. Offer the client water before the session begins, and have a glass of water with a flexible straw available during the session.

If the purpose of the treatment is to enhance the immune system during or before flu season, urge the client to have three to seven sessions in one week. While this frequency of sessions is very beneficial, it is intense, and mind-body reactions or healing crises are possible. Be sure to read the material on those subjects later in this text.

Students who are practicing this massage sequence may find it tedious to keep counting the seconds and numbers of circles. However, the results are worth the effort: This is a very delightful massage experience for the client. Not only does it stimulate lymph circulation, it is deeply relaxing. With appropriate music, soft lighting, subtle aromatherapy, and carefully selected emollient, as well as skillful, directed touch, the client perceives the work on more than one level and can find the experience profound.

LDM is performed on both sides of the neck and face at the same time, although the directions only mention one side. Use both hands and work both sides at the same time. *Unless otherwise indicated, use stationary circles. Each circle should last 7 seconds, and the circles should be repeated for a full minute, at least seven circles.*

STEP

BY

STEP

Treating the Neck

1. Gather equipment and supplies. Adjust the height of the table. Use a bolster, if needed, for the client's legs. If the room is cool, cover the client. Offer a drink of water.

2. Sit or stand at the client's head. Carefully drape a warm, moist towel over client's face, leaving room for the client to breathe. Allow the towel to cool to room temperature. As the towel cools, massage gently through the towel to relax the tissues. Before removing the towel, use it to gently wipe the face to prevent massaging any cosmetics or dirt particles into the skin.

3. Apply warm lotion to the skin with smooth strokes, covering the face and the front and back of the neck. Lotion or cream is optional, but it is recommended because some clients may worry about the skin being stretched or irritated, and the lotion or moisturizer is very soothing.

4. Begin with twenty stationary circles over the supraclavicular nodes, placing fingers above the upper margin of the clavicle. It takes nearly 3 minutes to massage this area.

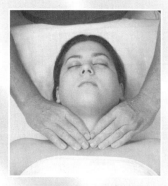

5. Perform twenty stationary circles on the subauricular nodes, between the ear and the mastoid process, posterior and inferior to the ear. Use three or four fingers, flat against the skin, to stretch the skin gently in a circular direction, counting each circle carefully to keep the pace very slow. This takes nearly 3 minutes.

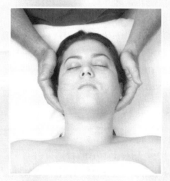

6. Drain the anterior cervical chain of nodes, along the region of the sternocleidomastoid muscle. Place all four fingers over the area from the bottom of the ear to the clavicle and very slowly stretch the skin in stationary circles seven times, counting 7 seconds for each circle. Repeat three times, taking about 3 minutes to massage the anterior cervical chain of nodes.

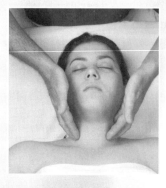

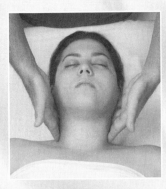

7. Repeat Step 6 on the posterior chain of cervical nodes.

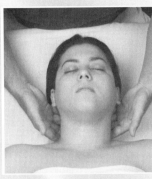

8. Slide the flat fingers of both hands under the neck, covering the skin from the bottom of the neck to the hairline. Perform seven stationary circles, moving the skin on the back of the neck over the cervical vertebrae.

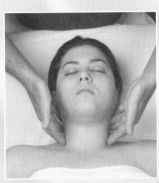

9. Place the flat fingers on the sides of the neck, between the ear and the collar, and perform stationary circles on the sides of the neck.

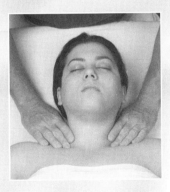

10. Place two flat fingers inside the triangle formed by the sternocleidomastoid muscle, the clavicle, and the scalene muscles, and again perform stationary circles for a full minute.

(continued)

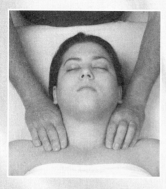

11. Place the fingertips along the upper border of the clavicle, and repeat the stationary circles.

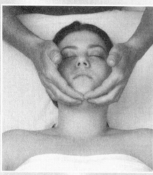

12. Move to the front of the neck. Place flat fingers under the chin, and massage for 1 minute.

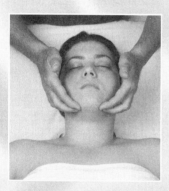

13. Move laterally to a position under the jaw line (midway between the chin and the angle of the jaw), and massage for 1 minute.

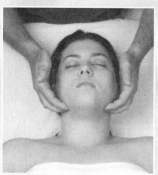

14. Place fingers on the neck immediately under the ear, and massage for 1 minute.

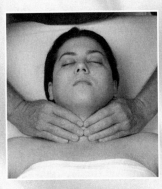

15. Place flat fingertips of both hands over the thyroid cartilage in the center of the neck (Adam's apple), and massage for 1 minute using the lightest pressure. Omit steps 15, 16, and 17 (the front of the neck) for any client who has thyroid abnormalities.

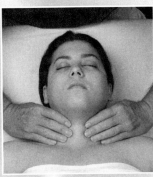

16. Place flat fingertips in the depression between the thyroid cartilage and the sternocleidomastoid muscles and massage using very light pressure.

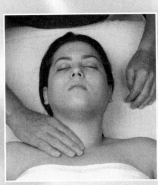

17. Place the flat fingertips of one hand in the central depression at the bottom of the throat between the two sternocleidomastoid muscles, and massage for 1 minute.

18. Effleurage the throat and the back of the neck.

STEP

BY

STEP

Working on the Face

The first section of the face takes about 15 minutes to complete.

1. Mist your hands with hydrosol or water (away from the client's face) to rehydrate the lotion or moisturizer. With warm hands, effleurage the face gently as an introduction to face work.

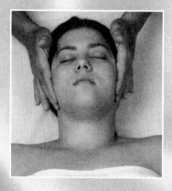

2. Place flat fingers over the region of the masseter muscle, at the angle of the jaw. Perform twenty stationary circles (nearly 3 minutes at 7 seconds per circle.)

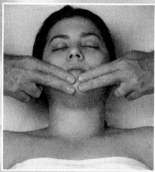

3. Using flat fingers as much as possible, perform stationary circles in sets of seven over the following regions, in order (each step takes nearly a minute):

   a. On the chin, below the bottom lip.

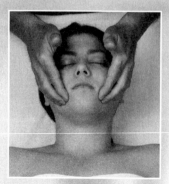

   b. Along the jaw line from the mouth to the angle of the jaw.

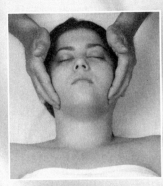

c. Over the angle of the jaw.

d. Over the upper lip, below the nose.

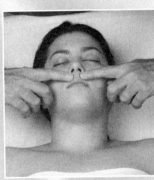

e. Over the corners of the mouth.

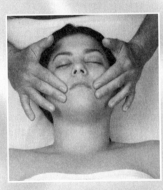

f. On the wings of the nose.

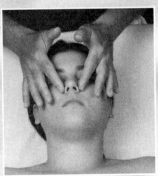

(continued)

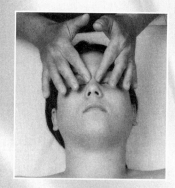

g. On the bridge of the nose (over the bony area of the middle of the nose).

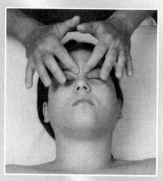

h. At the root of the nose (close to the eyes, but still on the bony protuberance of the nose).

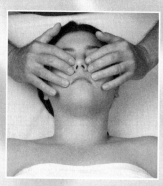

4. Place the tips of all four fingers in a curve from the medial corners of the eyes to the bottom of the nose, following the nasolabial groove or laugh lines. Massage for 1 minute.

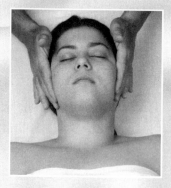

5. Place flat fingers over the region of the masseter muscle and massage seven circles, 7 seconds each.

The second section of the face takes nearly 10 minutes to complete.

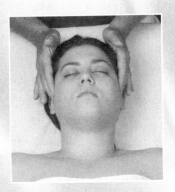

6. Place flat fingers over the preauricular nodes, in front of the ears. Begin with twenty circles, which takes nearly 3 minutes.

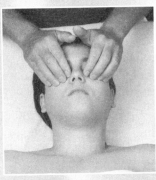

7. Around the eyes, place the tips of the fingers in a semicircle below the eye, as close to the eye socket as possible, without touching the eyes. Massage for 1 minute.

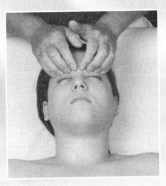

8. Place the flat fingers over the eyebrows. Curl the fingertips down below the eyebrows to massage the area above the eye socket as well. Massage for 1 minute.

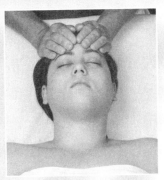

9. Place flat fingers of both hands on the forehead, and rest the palms of both hands on the scalp. Massage in larger circles, using the entire surface of each hand to move the skin of the forehead and scalp.

(continued)

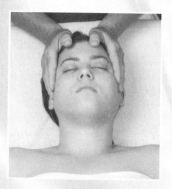

10. Place flat fingers over the temple, covering the area between the eyes and ears, resting the palms on the scalp over the temporalis muscle. Massage for 1 minute, using the entire surface of each hand. It might be tempting to apply firmer pressure here, but maintain the correct pressure and speed.

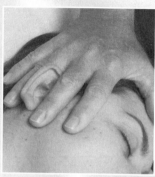

11. Place two flat fingers in front of the ears on each side, two fingers behind the ears in a fork position, and rest the palms of the hands on the scalp over the temporalis muscle. Massage for 1 minute.

12. Massage the scalp in large, gentle circles, moving the skin, for 2 or 3 minutes.

13. Massage each of the following areas for 1 to 3 minutes, until the lymph movement can be felt. If there are palpable changes in the tissues that show lymph drainage has increased, 1 minute will suffice. If lymph drainage is still sluggish or not palpable, up to 3 minutes on each location may be required.

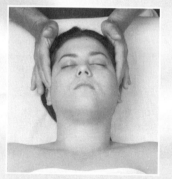

a. Preauricular nodes

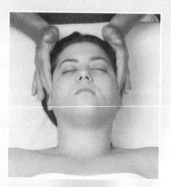

b. Angle of the jaw, over the masseter muscle

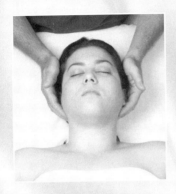

c. Posterior and inferior to the ear over the deep nodes

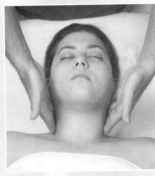

d. Posterior cervical chain

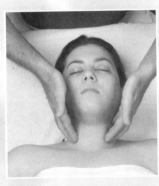

e. Anterior cervical chain

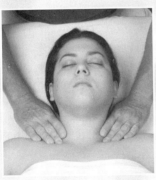

f. Along the superior border of the clavicle

(continued)

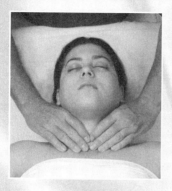

g. Above the medial ends of the clavicle

14. Gently effleurage the face and neck.

Use scalp massage to begin to waken the client. Gently tell the client that the massage is over and that it is time to awaken. Ask the client to turn on the side in the fetal position to stretch the lower back briefly before arising. Then, have the client sit on the table with the legs dangling toward the floor, to raise blood pressure and prevent fainting. Encourage yawning and stretching, which also stimulate lymph flow and raise blood pressure. After a few minutes, allow the client to stand. Be sure to stand at the client's side as he or she slides off the massage table and stands.

Lymph Drainage Massage on the Upper Extremities and Trunk

Identifying Upper Extremity and Trunk Indications

Edema of the upper extremity can arise from injury, repetitive motion strain, scar tissue, and more serious conditions, such as the scar tissue and obstruction that result from cancer surgery. It can sometimes result simply from the hand and arm hanging downward so that gravity pulls tissue fluid down the arm. All these conditions respond to lymph drainage massage. Scar tissue responds slowly to massage and takes repeated sessions to obtain visible results. Progress is faster if LDM is combined with connective tissue massage, such as skin rolling or cross-fiber friction.

Inflammation resulting from overuse, such as carpal tunnel syndrome, tennis elbow, and frozen shoulder, responds well to LDM. LDM speeds healing, reduces inflammation, reduces pain, and improves circulation and flexibility. Generally, clients with these conditions also need deeper massage on the overworked muscles to stretch and relax these muscles, and possibly movement training to change or eliminate the movement causing the problem.

LDM is indicated for painful, swollen breasts due to the hormone fluctuations of the menstrual cycle, pregnancy, or birth-control pills. It is important for women who wear constricting brassieres to perform self-massage on their breasts regularly. Because lymph vessels are close to the surface of the skin, tight bras that leave lines in the skin when removed are compressing lymph vessels, leading to sluggish or obstructed lymph flow. Over years, this can contribute to increased infections and other breast problems.

Locating Axillary and Breast Lymph Nodes

Lymph nodes of the upper quadrants and upper extremities (Figure 11–1) include the axillary nodes (central axillary nodes, pectoral nodes, subscapular nodes, and lateral nodes), the infraclavicular and supraclavicular nodes, and the internal mammary chain.

Most of the lymph fluid from the superficial tissues of the chest, breast, and upper extremity drains into the pectoral, subscapular, and lateral nodes and from those three groups into the central axillary nodes. From the central axillary nodes, fluid travels to the infraclavicular and supraclavicular nodes. Some of the lymph from the breast area drains into the internal mammary chain, then to the infraclavicular nodes.

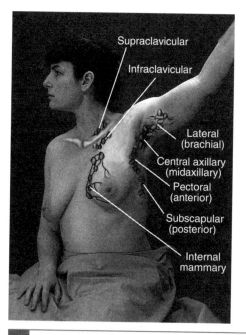

Figure 11–1 Regional lymphatics and drainage patterns of the upper quadrant.

Observing and Palpating Lymph Nodes

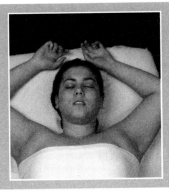

Axillary lymph nodes are easily located. With the client lying supine on the table, abduct rotate the arm so the arm is lying at an angle from the shoulder, the hand near the top of the head. If necessary, support the arm with a pillow so that the arm and shoulder are relaxed.

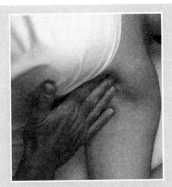

Locate the central axillary nodes by placing the fingers deep into the center of the axilla, and press the tissue gently against the thoracic wall. Massage in gentle circles to locate the nodes.

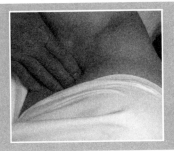

Locate the pectoral nodes behind the lateral edge of the pectoralis major (the anterior wall of the axilla).

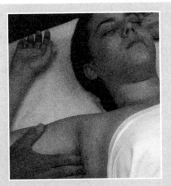

Locate the subscapular nodes at the anterior edge of the latissimus dorsi muscle (the posterior wall of the axilla.)

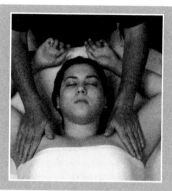

The brachial nodes are located on inner aspect of the arm, near the axilla, along the axillary vein.

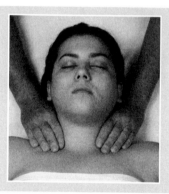

To locate the supraclavicular nodes, place the fingertips above the upper border of the clavicle, lateral to the origin of the sternocleidomastoid muscle. Massage in gentle, little circles.

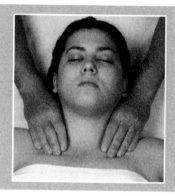

To locate the infraclavicular nodes, place the fingertips just below the lower border of the clavicle, and massage in gentle, little circles. In general, the nodes should not be easily palpable.

The nodes should not be painful to the touch, and they should be very small. Nodes that are enlarged and painful when palpated indicate infection, and the client should be referred to a physician. Likewise, enlarged nodes that are fixed, or immovable, indicate a possible serious health problem, and the client should be referred to a physician. Once the condition has been examined by a physician and serious health conditions have been ruled out, it is safe to proceed with the massage.

Supplies

- warm blanket
- small bolster under the knees
- small bolster or rolled hand towel under client's neck
- aromatherapy eye pillow or eye pads
- breast drape
- small pillow to support the arm, if necessary
- drinking water, with a flexible straw

Sequencing Upper Extremity and Trunk Lymph Drainage Massage

Clients who are accustomed to receiving full-body massages in one hour may be surprised to find that this cannot be done with LDM. Because the massage is very slow and it takes a long time to cover just one quadrant of the body, encourage clients to have at least three sessions of LDM: face and neck in the first session, upper body in the next session, and lower body in the final session.

Reducing lymph stasis, or stagnation, takes more time than moving lymph in an area with no obstruction. It may take several sessions over just one quadrant of the body to reduce edema when there is obstruction. If the client has no edema and is in reasonably good health, lymph will move more quickly and the massage will take less time, allowing the therapist to cover a larger area.

Treating the Trunk and Upper Extremities

Plan the massage carefully. Using the following basic outlines, the therapist can develop a step-by-step plan for the massage. When first learning LDM, it helps to have an instructor demonstrate exactly where to place the hands and for how long to massage each area. With experience the therapist will progress from following a detailed outline to more intuitive work, responding to tissue changes that indicate the therapy has succeeded.

Following the General Upper Quadrant and Extremity Procedure

Unless otherwise indicated, use stationary circles. Each circle should last 7 seconds and should be repeated for 1 minute.

1. With the client in a supine position, massage the following lymph nodes first:

   a Supraclavicular and infraclavicular

   b. Axillary

2. Massage the anterior trunk quadrant adjacent to the lymph nodes.

   a. Begin proximal to the nodes and work toward the midline and lower margin of the ribs.

3. Massage proximal to distal on the limb.

   a. Massage from the shoulder to the hand and fingers.

   b. Massage from the hand to the shoulder, which should take less time, because, if the previous work has been done well, lymph circulation will have increased and the therapist will be able to feel the lymph move.

4. Help the client turn over to a prone position.

5. Massage the posterior trunk quadrant, beginning close to the lymph nodes and working outward, toward the midline and the lower margin of the ribs.

6. Massage the posterior surface of the limb.

   a. On the upper extremity, massage any areas that were not massaged from the front.

7. Help the client again turn over to a supine position.

8. Massage over the axillary lymph nodes, then the infraclavicular and supraclavicular nodes again, to complete this quadrant.

9. Finish with gentle effleurage.

Detailing the Upper Quadrant and Extremity Procedure

1. Gather equipment and supplies. Help the client onto the table, and drape warmly. Offer water, cover the eyes with aromatherapy eye pillow or eye pads. Begin with the client in the supine position.

2. Standing at the client's side, massage the lymph nodes first.

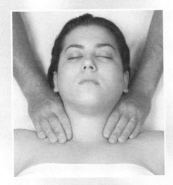

   a. *Supraclavicular nodes:* Place the pads of the fingers just above the clavicle, lateral to the origin of the sternocleidomastoid muscle. Using light pressure and moving the skin in slow circles, massage for about 3 minutes.

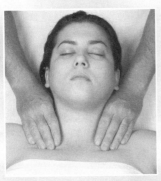

   b. *Infraclavicular nodes:* Place the pads of the fingers along the lower margin of the clavicle and massage using stationary circles for $2^{1}/_{2}$ to 3 minutes.

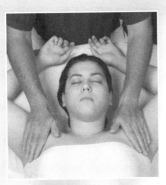

   c. *Brachial nodes:* With the client's arm raised above the head and supported on a pillow, if necessary, place the entire hand over the brachial nodes and massage for at least 1 minute.

(continued)

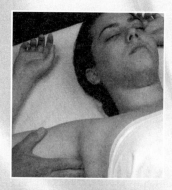

d. *Subscapular nodes:* Place the fingertips beneath the latissimus dorsi muscle at the back wall of the axilla and massage for at least 1 minute.

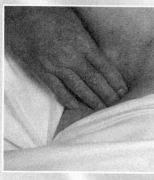

e. *Pectoral nodes:* Place the fingertips beneath the pectoralis major muscle at the front wall of the axilla and massage for at least 1 minute.

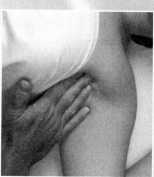

f. *Central axillary nodes:* Place the fingers at the apex of the axilla between the pectoralis major and the latissimus dorsi muscle. Massage using stationary circles for 2½ to 3 minutes.

3. Massage the anterior trunk quadrant adjacent to the lymph nodes. Begin proximal to the nodes and work toward the midline and the lower margin of the ribs. At each step, massage for about 1 minute, using stationary circles. Count 7 seconds per circle.

a. Place a flat hand over the shoulder joint between the deltoid muscle and breast.

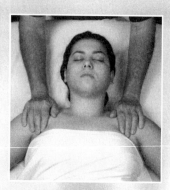

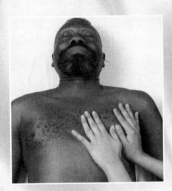

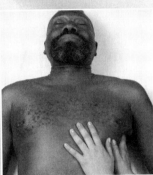

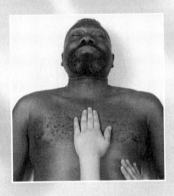

b. Massage the area of the pectoralis major. For a male client, simply place both flat hands to cover the upper portion of the pectoralis major and massage for 1 minute. Then, use both hands to cover the lower portion of the pectoralis major, below the nipple, and massage for 1 minute. Place one hand over the sternum and massage for 1 minute.

(continued)

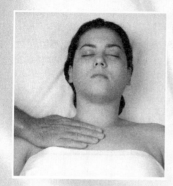

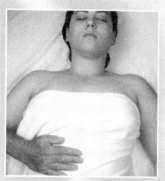

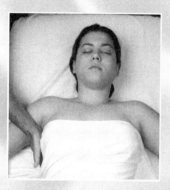

c. For a female client, place one hand along the lower margin of the clavicle, above the breast, and massage for 1 minute. Place one hand over the sternum and massage for 1 minute. Place one hand below the breast and massage for 1 minute. Place one hand on the lateral margin of the breast (ask the client to move the breast tissue out of the way) and massage for 1 minute. (The female breast will definitely benefit from breast massage. However, in many places in the United States, it is illegal for massage therapists to touch the female breast. Before or after the session, explain and demonstrate self-massage so that the client can do it herself at home.)

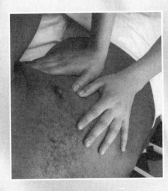

d. Use one or two hands to massage the lower rib cage for 1 minute.

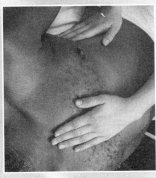

e. Use one or two hands to cover the lateral wall of the thorax between the bottom of the ribs and the axilla and massage for 1 minute.

4. Massage from proximal to distal on the limb using stationary circles for at least 1 minute over each of the following areas:

a. Deltoid muscle area (cap of the shoulder)

b. Front of the upper arm, over the biceps brachii muscle

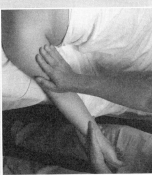

(continued)

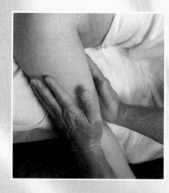

c. Front of the upper arm, on the tissue on both sides of the biceps brachii muscle

d. Medial and lateral ends of elbow crease

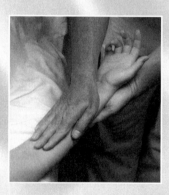

e. Lower arm

f. Palm of the hand

g. Pads of the proximal phalanges of the fingers and thumb

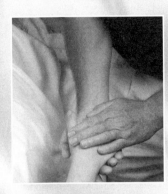

h. Massage the dorsum of the hand

i. Reverse the previous steps and massage from the hand to the shoulder

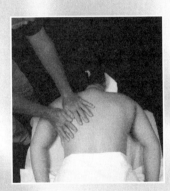

5. Help the client turn over to a prone position.

6. Massage the posterior trunk quadrant, beginning close to the lymph nodes and working outward toward the midline and the lower margin of the ribs. Massage each of the following:

a. Shoulder joint

b. Lateral edge of scapula

c. Scapula

d. Back of the neck

e. Upper trapezius

f. Middle trapezius

g. Lower trapezius

(continued)

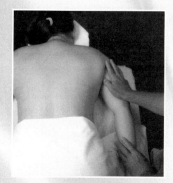

h. The triceps muscle, using one or both hands

i. Posterior aspect of the lower arm

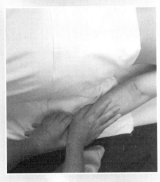

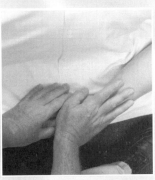

j. The supraclavicular and infraclavicular nodes by placing the hand over the trapezius muscle at the top of the shoulder and curving the fingers under to reach the clavicle

7. Help the client turn over again to a supine position.

8. Massage over the axillary lymph nodes, then the infraclavicular and supraclavicular nodes again, to complete this quadrant.

9. Finish with gentle effleurage.

STEP

BY

STEP

Conducting Breast Self-Massage

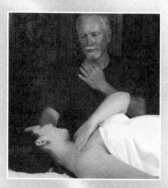

1. Seated in a chair or lying supine in bed, place the fingertips above the clavicle and massage in gentle slow circles for 1 minute.

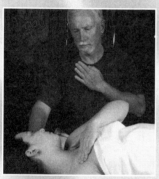

2. Repeat under the clavicle for 1 minute.

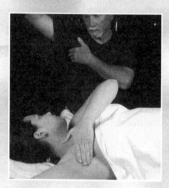

3. With the arm raised comfortably above the head, use the fingers and palm to massage the axilla in gentle, slow circles for a minute or more.

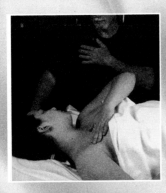

4. Place the palm and fingers above the breast and below the clavicle and massage for 1 minute in slow, gentle circles.

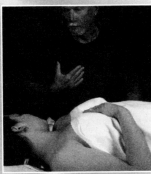

5. Place the hand over the sternum and massage for 1 minute.

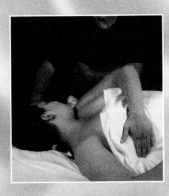

6. Place the hand under the breast on the ribs and massage for 1 minute.

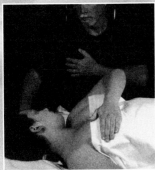

7. Place the hand at the side of the rib cage, below the axilla, and massage for 1 minute.

(continued)

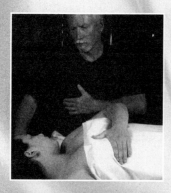

8. Repeat this pattern on the breast. Massage the upper portion of the breast for 1 minute, then the medial side, then the bottom of the breast, then the lateral side of the breast.

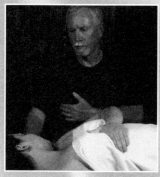

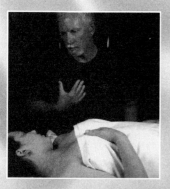

9. Massage the axillary nodes again.

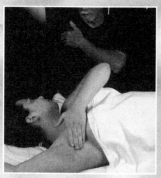

10. Massage the infraclavicular and supraclavicular nodes again.

11. Repeat on the other breast.

Addressing Obstructive Edema of the Upper Extremity

There are too few LDM therapists in the United States to treat the number of people with obstructive edema or lymphedema. Lymphedema is a progressive disorder that cannot be cured, although it does respond well to LDM, bandaging, and exercise, often called comprehensive decongestive therapy. Ideally, clients with lymphedema would be referred by their physicians to therapists with advanced training in these areas. While this is not always the case, more and more physicians and more qualified therapists are becoming aware of LDM's benefits.

Beginning massage therapists are able to help clients with obstructive edema using basic LDM. For the best results, work under the supervision of the client's physician, and teach the client how to perform self-massage. For more serious edema, the sequence of the massage differs somewhat. It is necessary to massage the well side first and to encourage movement of lymph from the congested side across the watershed to lymph nodes on the opposite side.

To perform the massage, divide the trunk into quadrants, then massage:

1. The cervical, axillary, and inguinal lymph nodes on both sides of the trunk.

2. The trunk quadrants adjacent to the quadrant of the edematous limb. For instance, for an edematous left arm, massage the right-upper quadrant and the left-lower quadrant of the trunk.

3. The trunk quadrant closest to the edematous limb (in this example, the left-upper quadrant).

4. The proximal area of the edematous limb (in this example, the upper arm from the shoulder to the elbow).

5. The distal areas of the edematous limb (following this example, the lower arm and hand).

6. From the fingers back up to the shoulder.

7. The lymph nodes again.

8. Repeat as often as needed to produce a palpable change in the edematous tissues. It is safe to perform LDM daily, although daily sessions should be limited to an hour and a half at the most to prevent nausea, dizziness, and other symptoms.

Lymph Drainage Massage on the Lower Extremities and Trunk

Identifying Indications and Contraindications on the Lower Extremities and Trunk

Edema of the lower leg can be due to injury, repetitive-motion strain, scar tissue, and more serious conditions, such as the scar tissue and obstruction that result from cancer surgery. It can sometimes be caused simply by the position of the leg and foot, for example, when sitting for a long time without moving, tissue fluid pools in the lower leg. Edema of the lower limb can also be due to obstruction from the weight gain of pregnancy or obesity or tight clothing such as socks or stockings. All these conditions respond to LDM.

Edema of the lower leg is an indication for LDM. LDM moves fluid out of the tissue spaces into the lymphatic vessels from whence it can be returned to the bloodstream. LDM also improves the appearance and texture of the skin, which can become stiff, coarse, and reddened because of chronic edema.

However, edema is also a symptom of a variety of serious illnesses, such as congestive heart failure and kidney failure. Edema of the legs and hands should be referred to a physician to rule out serious underlying illnesses before proceeding, unless the cause of the edema is obvious, such as a long period of enforced sitting on a plane, for instance, or a known side effect of medication.

If a client has been sitting for a long time on a long car ride or flight, a blood clot is possible. If the lower leg is inflamed, red, hot, painful, and swollen, do not massage. If there is sharp pain, do not massage. In either case, refer to a physician to rule out a blood clot.

Before beginning to massage, look for varicose veins. If these are inflamed and painful, no massage should be given until the condition has been examined by a physician. If the veins are not painful and are not red, hot, and swollen, light massage like LDM is safe. It is generally safe to massage over spider veins and small broken capillaries.

LDM helps speed healing of injuries by stimulating microcirculation, assisting in the removal of cellular debris from the site of the injury, and making room for nutrients from increased blood flow to the area. Massaging as soon as safe after an injury minimizes the amount of scar tissue that forms and it improves tissue structure.

Even old scars can benefit from LDM, which can help scars to become softer, smoother, and more flexible. Progress is slow, however, so it is a good idea to teach clients to self-treat daily. A combination of connective tissue massage, such as deep-tissue massage or myofascial release with LDM, produces the best results.

Locating Inguinal Lymph Nodes

Lymph nodes for the abdomen and lower extremities are in the femoral triangle, bounded by the inguinal ligament and the sartorius and adductor muscles (Figure 12–1). The femoral artery is in the femoral angle with the

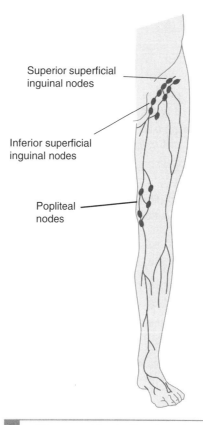

Superior superficial
inguinal nodes

Inferior superficial
inguinal nodes

Popliteal
nodes

Figure 12–1 The inguinal lymph nodes.

lymph nodes. There are two chains of lymph nodes, one near the inguinal ligament, called the horizontal or superior chain, and the other along the femoral vein, called the vertical or inferior chain. A small group of nodes, called the popliteal nodes, is near the medial knee.

These lymph nodes receive fluid from the superficial tissues of the abdomen, the lower back and gluteal regions, and the legs (Figure 12–2). Lymph from the abdominal region drains inferiorly, toward the inguinal nodes. Lymph from the gluteal region drains laterally around the hips to the inguinal nodes. Lymph from the lower extremities drains superiorly to the inguinal nodes. However, on the back of the thigh, lymph from the medial side drains medially, around to the front of the thigh and up to the inguinal nodes. Lymph from the lateral side of the posterior thigh drains laterally, around to the front of the thigh and up to the inguinal nodes.

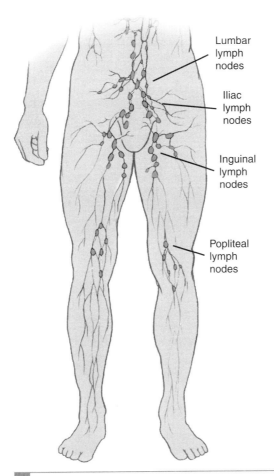

Lumbar lymph nodes

Iliac lymph nodes

Inguinal lymph nodes

Popliteal lymph nodes

Figure 12–2 Location of the lower quadrant nodes.

Observing and Palpating the Inguinal Lymph Nodes

Help the client lie on the table in a supine position, with the knees slightly flexed. Locate the inguinal ligament and the sartorius and rectus femoris muscles. Lymph nodes are located inferior to the inguinal ligament in the depression medial to the muscles. Rest flat fingers gently on the femoral triangle and wait a few seconds to feel the femoral pulse. Using flat fingertips, gently massage over the femoral triangle to locate the lymph nodes. Small lymph nodes that move with the skin are normal. Enlarged, tender lymph nodes indicate an infection or another disease process. Discontinue the massage and refer the client to a physician to rule out infection.

Supplies

- bottom sheet
- top sheet
- warm blanket
- small bolster under the knees
- small bolster or rolled hand towel under the client's neck
- aromatherapy eye pillow or eye pads
- drinking water with a flexible straw

Conducting Lymph Drainage Massage on the Lower Extremities and Trunk

Unless otherwise indicated, use stationary circles. Each circle should last 7 seconds and should be repeated for 1 minute.

1. With the client in a prone position, massage the inguinal lymph nodes.

2. Massage the anterior trunk quadrant between the inguinal ligament and the umbilicus (navel), from the midline to the side.

3. Massage the lower limb proximal to distal, from the inguinal ligament to the foot and toes.

4. Work back toward the lymph nodes again, massaging distal to proximal.

5. Help the client turn over to a prone position.

6. Massage the posterior trunk quadrant from the gluteal crease to the waist, from the sacrum laterally to the great trochanter.

7. Massage the posterior surface of the lower limb, from the inguinal ligament to the foot and toes.

8. Help the client turn over again to a prone position.

9. Massage over the lymph nodes again to complete this quadrant.

STEP

BY

STEP

Completing the Detailed Procedure

1. Gather equipment and supplies. Help the client onto the table and drape warmly. Place a small bolster under the client's knees and a small pillow under the ankle of the leg to be massaged.

2. Standing at one side, massage the inguinal nodes about 3 minutes.

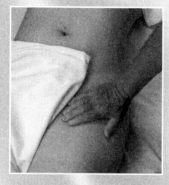

3. Work the abdomen in a fan-shaped pattern. Place the hands over the abdomen between the inguinal ligament and navel with the finger tips along the midline and the heels of the hands near the inguinal ligament. Using both hands, move the skin of the abdomen in large, slow circles.

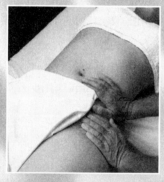

4. Move the hands so that the finger tips are along the waist and the heels of the hands are close to the inguinal ligament. Massage as before for 1 minute.

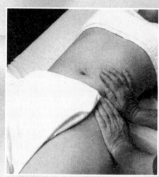

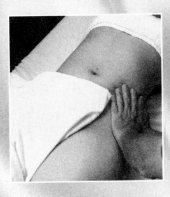

5. Move the hands so that the finger tips reach down the side close to the massage table, between the waist and hip joint, with the heels of the hands near the inguinal ligament as before. Massage for 1 minute.

6. If necessary, repeat abdominal massage until there is a palpable change in the tissue.

7. Massage along the "side seam" of the thigh. Place the hands over the upper third of the iliotibial band, near the hip joint, and massage for about 1 minute.

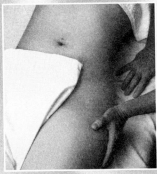

8. Place the hands over the middle third of the iliotibial band, and massage for 1 minute.

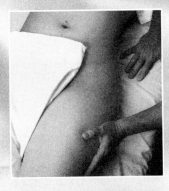

9. Place the hands over the lower third of the iliotibial band, near the knee, and massage for 1 minute.

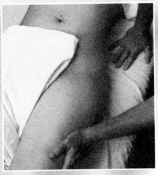

(continued)

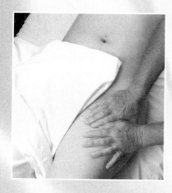

10. Massage along the front of the thigh from the inguinal crease to the knee. Place the hands over the upper third of the anterior thigh, inferior to the inguinal crease, covering the upper rectus femoris muscle, and massage for 1 minute.

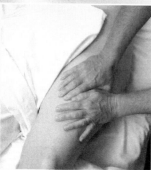

11. Place the hands at about the midpoint of the anterior thigh, and repeat circles.

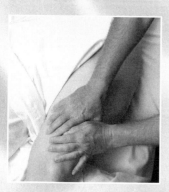

12. Place the hands superior to the knee, and repeat circles.

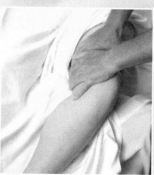

13. Roll the knee out slightly, away from the midline, to make access to the inner thigh easier. Place the hands over the lower half of the medial thigh, and massage for 1 minute.

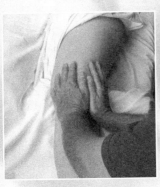

14. Place the hands around knee and use a scooping motion to move fluid toward the inguinal nodes. A "scoop" is a semicircle. Each scoop should take seven seconds, and should be repeated seven times. Place one hand on each side of the knee, compress slightly, and stretch the skin in a semicircle toward the lymph nodes. Then, release the pressure and return to the point of origin.

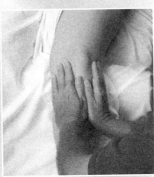

15. Working from the knee to the ankles, use a scooping motion with one or both hands to move fluid toward the nodes. It will take three or four steps, repeating the movements seven times at each step, or about 4 minutes total for the lower leg.

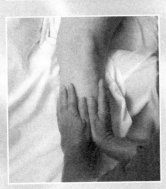

(continued)

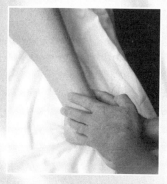

16. Using flat fingers, perform stationary circles around the bony protuberances of the ankles.

17. Complete stationary circles on the dorsum (top) of the foot.

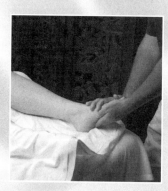

18. Using a very slow, scooping motion with the thumb and forefinger, massage each toe seven times for about 1 minute per toe.

19. Reverse the preceding steps to work back up the leg to the inguinal nodes. Continue using slow, stationary circles or scooping movements.

20. Massage over the inguinal nodes using stationary circles twenty times, for about 3 minutes.

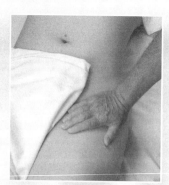

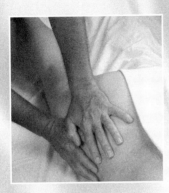

21. Help the client turn over to a prone position, and drape warmly. If the client desires, place a small pillow or rolled towel under the ankle joints.

22. Using flat hands, massage the gluteal region in a fan-shaped pattern. Place the hands so that the heels of the hands are close to the hip joint with the fingers parallel to the gluteal crease. Massage for 1 minute.

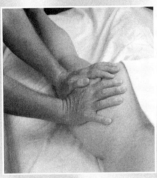

23. Place the hands so that the heels of the hands are close to the hip joint with the fingers pointing toward the sacrum, and massage for 1 minute.

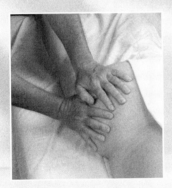

24. Place the hands so that the heels of the hands are close to the hip joint with the fingers pointing toward the waist, parallel to the massage table. Massage for 1 minute.

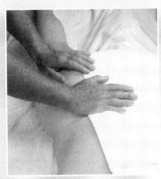

25. Massage the lumbar region.

(continued)

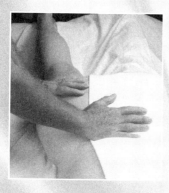

26. Massage over the sacrum.

27. Complete stationary circles over the back of the knee to open the popliteal nodes.

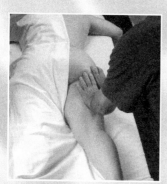

28. Place flat hands on the upper thigh, just below the gluteal crease. Massage for 1 minute.

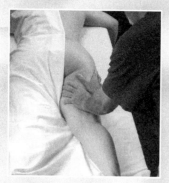

29. Place flat hands mid-thigh, with the fingers of each hand reaching down to the massage table on each side. Massage for 1 minute, moving the skin in a semicircle up toward the inguinal crease and out to the sides of the thigh.

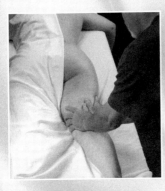

30. Place flat hands just above the knee on the lower thigh, with fingers reaching to the massage table on each side. Move the skin in a semicircle up toward the inguinal crease and out to the sides of the thigh.

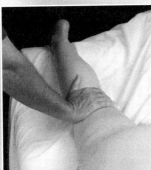

31. Massage the back of the knee, using stationary circles, for 1 minute.

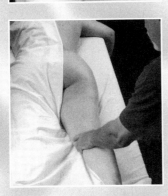

32. Place flat hands just below the knee on the upper calf, with fingers reaching to the massage table on each side. Move the skin in a semicircle up toward the knee and out to the sides of the calf.

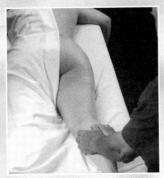

33. Repeat at the midpoint of the calf.

(continued)

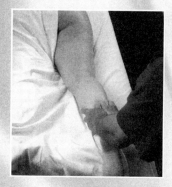

34. Repeat at the bottom of the calf seven times.

35. Using flat fingers, perform stationary circles around the bony protuberances of the ankles for 1 minute.

36. Repeat on the soles of the feet.

37. Reverse the preceding directions and work back up the legs to the gluteal crease.

38. Help the client turn over into a supine position. Drape warmly. Finish the lower quadrant by massaging over the inguinal nodes again in 20 circles.

39. Help the client into the fetal position to stretch the lower back. Then, help the client sit. Use percussion or neck and shoulder massage to invigorate the client. Stand next to client as the client climbs off the massage table to prevent falling. If the client is very groggy, walk with the client, offer water, turn on the lights, open windows, and so on to help the client to awaken fully. Do not allow a client to leave until the client is fully awake and able to drive safely.

Treating Obstructive Edema with Lymph Drainage Massage

Divide the trunk into quadrants.

1. Massage the cervical, axillary, and inguinal lymph nodes on both sides of the trunk.

2. Massage the trunk quadrant adjacent to the quadrant of the edematous limb. For instance, for an edematous left leg, massage the left-upper quadrant and the right-lower quadrant of the trunk.

3. Massage the trunk quadrant closest to the edematous limb (in this example, massage the left-lower quadrant).

4. Massage the proximal area of the edematous limb (in this example, massage the upper thigh then the lower thigh).

5. Massage the distal areas of the edematous limb (in this example, massage the knee, calf, then foot of the left-lower leg).

6. Work back toward the lymph nodes.

7. Finish by massaging the lymph nodes again.

8. Repeat as often as needed to produce a palpable change in the edematous tissues.

Cellulite

Cellulite, or lipedema, is a controversial subject. It does or does not exist according to whom one consults. Although medical practitioners do not acknowledge cellulite's existence by and large, practitioners in the massage, beauty, and skin-care industries think it is real, treat it as if it were real, and achieve positive outcomes.

Introducing Cellulite

Cellulite is an unscientific, descriptive term. It was first used in Sweden at the end of the nineteenth century and was adopted by French salons to refer to the dimpled, rippling, subcutaneous deposits of fat, body fluids, and waste materials that form on the bodies of many women and some men. Another term for the condition is lipedema. This can be misleading because lipedema is not a true edema, consisting as it does of mostly fat cells and connective tissue. However, chronic lipedema can eventually develop into true edema along with chronic inflammation, resulting in changes in the skin—making it thicker, coarse, less flexible, red, and dry.

Cellulite most commonly appears on the hips, the thighs, and the upper arms. On older women it may also appear across the upper back, across the abdomen, and even on the calves. To the touch, the texture of cellulite is lumpy and discontinuous, and when squeezed or palpated cellulite comes to the hand in lumps and masses. The appearance of cellulite is unfortunate at the least and positively disfiguring in severe cases. The tendency toward cellulite can be inherited, although lifestyle and diet play a major role in its formation.

Cellulite should be differentiated from obesity. In cellulite, fat cells are normal, but the connective tissue is damaged, which contributes to the rippled and lumpy appearance of the skin. Cellulite is distributed mainly in the well-known "saddlebag" area, over the hips, abdomen, and thighs. Other areas of the body are normal in size and appearance. Cellulite has two components: an unattractive distribution of fat cells below the waist and a disturbance of the connective tissue, which causes scarring and distortion of the superficial fascia. Cellulite can also include true edema, which is an abnormal accumulation of fluid in these regions. Manual therapies are effective in treating the scarring of the connective tissue and the edema but cannot remove or redistribute fat cells.

Obesity is an abnormal accumulation of fat cells. It is not located only in the saddlebag area below the waist, but is distributed over the entire body. LDM cannot reduce the amount or size of fat stored in the body. However, over time the seriously obese patient will develop edema in the lower extremities marked by pitting edema and pathological changes to the skin. Because chronic edema can develop into more serious conditions, such as chronic infections or even some forms of cancer, it is important to treat the edema. The condition cannot be successfully cured unless the obesity is also addressed.

Cellulite forms in the superficial fascia, a layer of connective tissue below the skin that contains fat cells. Superficial fascia is fibrous and, due to inactivity, injuries, and improper exercise, adhesions (scar tissue) in the fascia can form, contributing to the bunched-up or rippled look of the skin. Not only does the superficial fascia become more fibrous, thickened, coarse, and less flexible, but it can also adhere to underlying structures that it normally slides over.

Improper exercise is also a factor in cellulite. Lack of exercise causes one set of problems, including weak muscles, poor skin tone, sluggish lymph circulation, and weight gain. Overexercise causes another set of problems: tense, overworked muscles contributing to fatigue and the buildup of the by-products of the combustion of energy. Overworked, fatigued muscles are easily injured, leading to tears in the connective tissue that in turn lead to the development of scar tissue and adhesions. Excessive exercise combined with very strict dieting can lead to malnutrition, which adversely affects the appearance and texture of the skin.

Obesity, sun, gravity, and exposure to cold can cause changes in the skin ranging from atrophy to hypertrophy. If the collagen of the skin is damaged, changes take place including accumulations of fat cells and thickened skin. Fat cells can change in size depending on exercise and diet. All of these conditions contribute to the appearance of cellulite.

Remedying Cellulite

In a nutshell, cellulite (lipedema) is a condition of stagnation, whatever the cause. The ultimate remedy is to enhance the body's circulation, improve nutrition, increase metabolism, and reduce scar tissue and adhesions in the superficial fascia. Treatment of cellulite requires more than just LDM. A successful program has to include changes in diet and lifestyle.

Treating the Body

The most effective body work treatment of cellulite combines connective tissue massage, or myofascial release, to break down adhesions in the superficial tissues and increase nutrition to the tissues, with gentle lymphatic massage to remove inflammation and toxins.

Deep tissue massage and myofascial release focus on connective tissue. The deep, slow massage strokes produce their effect by creating micro-tears in the superficial fascia. This makes tissue longer, smoother, and more flexible. The deep massage work also releases adhesions in the superficial fascia so that tissue moves more freely and no longer adheres to underlying structures. Deep massage followed by LDM and appropriate stretching makes the superficial fascia smoother, longer, and more flexible.

Creating tears in the superficial fascia with deep-tissue massage or myofascial release triggers the inflammatory response. Blood flow increases and capillaries become more permeable, thereby increasing nutrition to the tissues. Increased blood flow increases the amount of interstitial fluid, which in turn washes the cells and picks up microorganisms and foreign particles. LDM stimulates the removal of these toxins through the lymphatic system.

In this context, it is important to note that although superficial lymphatic capillaries are connected to deeper vessels via pathways through the adipose (fatty) tissue, they provide very little effective drainage of the fat cells. It is inaccurate to let clients believe that massage will remove or decrease fat cells. What body work *will* do is greatly improve the condition and appearance of the skin, reduce troublesome adhesions and scars, and increase the circulation of nutrients to tissues. As a result of the body work, the body will repair itself and move to a higher level of health and appearance.

The most successful treatment that actually removes fat cells from the body and restructures the shape of the body is liposuction. Liposuction can be used to remove fat cells and reshape the saddlebags where fat cells have accumulated. However the procedure itself damages the connective tissue, blood vessels, and lymph vessels in the area of the surgery. This can create more scarring if the procedure is not performed skillfully and if there is no follow-up. Scarring due to liposuction can cause edema, and chronic edema can lead to a worsening of the appearance of the skin, rather than improvement.

Clients who want to have liposuction should research carefully and select physicians who are experienced and who have a history of obtaining good results. It is important to select a physician who is interested, not only in doing the surgery, but also in educating the client to obtain the best possible result.

Once the surgery has healed, LDM is recommended because it can help the proper development of scar tissue, improve circulation, and assist in the removal of damaged tissues and chemicals. Deep-tissue massage is not recommended until the area has completely healed and there is no tenderness.

Having a Healthy Lifestyle

Whether or not the client chooses liposuction surgery or manual therapies, proper exercise is an important factor in obtaining good results. A good exercise regimen is to work out strenuously three days a week, stretch appropriately for one's own body two days a week, and rest for two days. Besides strengthening the cardiovascular system, strenuous exercise accomplishes two notable outcomes: (1) it builds and shapes muscles; and (2) it causes the body to use up energy stored in fat cells thereby reducing their size. Stretching lengthens and relaxes muscles so that they stay elastic, work more easily, and are less likely to be injured. Regular rest is important for healing and preventing injuries. Healing and growth take place during rest. The combination of strengthening exercises, stretching, and adequate rest will contribute to the best outcome in cellulite treatment.

Many people are imbalanced in their choice of exercise, preferring to do only vigorous exercise or only stretching. Some never exercise, thinking that their work is exercise enough, which is not true. If this is the case with the client who is seeking treatment for cellulite, encourage the client to get training from a personal trainer, a gym, an exercise video, or other training to balance the physical workout with stretching and rest.

Eating Properly

Finally, diet is essential to reducing cellulite (lipedema) and preventing it from returning. Proper nutrition and exercise reduce the size of fat cells. Encourage clients to avoid caffeine, sugar, refined flours, and heavy meats. Encourage them to think of fruit as cleansing, especially fruits high in vitamin C (which is a diuretic and stimulates the body to eliminate toxins through the kidneys). Encourage them to think of vegetables as healing, since they are full of fiber as well as vitamins and minerals.

Educate clients to understand that protein is fuel, and protein is found abundantly in *unrefined carbohydrates,* including whole grains, beans and legumes (peas, lentils, etc.) as well as meat. It is helpful to view meat as medicine, taken occasionally to strengthen. Meat provides concentrated energy for periods of very low strength, and also contains iron and complete proteins.

Meat can be strengthening and reduces pain, but like medicine, meat has side effects. It generally contains fat that is not healthful for humans, and meat is often full of chemicals to which the animal was exposed. Like humans, animals who are exposed to excessive amounts of toxins in their food, air, and water store those excess toxins in their muscles, fat cells, and organs. Eating meat means consuming the toxins stored in the meat. It makes sense to limit the amount of meat that is consumed and to eat only unadulterated meat raised by local farmers or organic meat from health food stores.

Fats, too, are necessary. They assist with absorbing nutrients in food and provide the precursor molecules to many hormones that are necessary to endocrine health. A diet completely without fat leads to malnutrition. A sign of malnutrition in an otherwise healthy-appearing individual is rough, dry skin with no elasticity. On palpation the skin feels grainy and dry, as if there were sand under the surface. The skin does not return to its normal condition after being stretched by a massage stroke, but remains bunched up.

If the therapist is not a nutritionist, he or she can still help clients eat better by encouraging all clients to learn more about food and diet in general, rather than giving them a specific diet to follow. Recommend books and newsletters that will give the clients the basics of good nutrition. The more clients know about nutrition, the better the choices they are likely to make in their diet.

Water is the drink of choice. It takes fluid to make the lymphatic system work, and most people, it can safely be said, do not drink enough water. Many beverages that are regularly consumed throughout the day, like coffee, tea, alcohol, and colas, are diuretic, contributing to dehydration and negatively affecting the circulation of lymph. Let clients know that by the time they feel thirsty they are already somewhat dehydrated. Drink regularly throughout the day without waiting to feel thirsty, and without forcing excessive amounts of fluids. A useful rule of thumb is to drink an ounce of water for every two pounds of body weight during the day. This rule reminds larger people to drink more water to keep their larger frames hydrated.

Summarizing Cellulite Treatment

To summarize, the following recommendations may be given to clients who are worried about cellulite:

Exercise

- Regular, vigorous exercise three times per week, including cardio-vascular and resistance exercise. The assistance of a personal trainer is highly recommended.

- Exercise such as stretching or yoga twice a week.

- Rest two days per week. Meditation, massage, breath work, guided imagery, and similar technologies are highly recommended for producing a restful, healing state of mind.

Body Work

- Regular connective tissue massage or myofascial release, and LDM. Note that deep massage techniques should not be applied to the same area of the body more than once every third day. LDM, however, may be given daily.

- Encourage clients to commit to a series of body work sessions, such as six in two weeks, to begin the cellulite work. Then suggest less frequent body work sessions while the client works on changing diet and exercise to maintain the progress achieved by the body work.

Diet

- Healthier diet that eliminates or reduces caffeine, sugar, refined carbohydrates, and red meats as much as possible. Rather than recommending a specific diet, encourage clients to learn more about nutrition.

- Plenty of fluids, especially water. A good rule of thumb is to drink at least one ounce of water per two pounds of body weight on a daily basis.

- Plenty of fruits and vegetables. Periodic internal cleansing with lettuce soup or vegetable and fruit juices.

Understanding Body Wraps

Body wraps work by inducing sweating. Despite various claims made in advertising, they are not effective in reducing cellulite because fat cells and connective tissue are not affected by sweating. Body wraps are diuretic: they cause water loss. They are not recommended for anyone who drinks a lot of diuretic beverages like coffee, tea, and cola. Because body wraps increase internal temperature, they are also not recommended for anyone with high blood pressure or anyone who is pregnant. Body wraps are not a good idea for anyone with serious claustrophobia.

However, having said this, body wraps are still a nice add-on service to offer with cellulite treatment. Seaweed, clay, and herbal wraps are exfoliating and improve the appearance and feel of the skin. Depending on the herbs used, herbal wraps can be stimulating or soothing. Aromatherapy wraps also can be soothing or stimulating and energizing, depending on the essential oils used. Body wraps are especially beneficial because they create an artificial fever, which stimulates lymph and blood circulation and increases the number of immune cells while slowing down the reproduction of bacteria and viruses.

The combination of connective tissue massage, LDM, and a body wrap can trigger a healing crisis. Limit the total amount of time in each session to no more than one and a half hours. Any client who is making big lifestyle changes toward better nutrition and better exercise is also likely to have a healing crisis, especially if receiving all these services in one session. If the client seems likely to have a healing crisis, limit the total amount of time and the number of services. Body wraps, deep tissue massage, and LDM can be spread out through several sessions with good results. Therapists should be familiar with the material later in this text on the concept of the healing crisis and should prepare their clients for the possibility of feeling flulike symptoms after cellulite treatment.

Treating Cellulite with Lymph Drainage Massage

Gather materials: oil or cream, bolster for knees, small roll to place under neck, small blanket or towel for warmth. For connective tissue massage, use little or no lubricant. Choose lotion that is quickly absorbed or an oil (like coconut oil) that is thin and has more drag than glide. Use sparingly. Cellulite creams such as those containing arnica and ivy may be applied at the end of the session.

Before beginning the session, ask the client to stand, wearing only underwear or a bathing suit. Examine cellulite. Observe the contour of the hips and legs, the texture and condition of the skin, and any markings including scar tissue, moles, lumps, etc. To measure progress, the therapist may want to measure the circumference of the hips and thighs, marking the level where the measurement is taken with a nontoxic, waxy pencil such as eyeliner. Another way to record the measurement is to measure the distance from a landmark like the knee crease (e.g., 7 inches above the posterior knee crease).

The therapist may also wish to take pictures of the area to be worked. However, photos should not be taken without prior permission from the client, and at the end of the treatment period the photographs should be returned to the client.

Explain the procedure to the client, so there are no surprises or unanswered questions. Assist the client onto the massage table, in a prone position. Drape warmly, and uncover the area to be massaged.

Assess the condition of the skin: color, texture, temperature, moisture, and elasticity. Look at the contour of the hips and legs. Look for skin thickening, ridges, lumps, and wrinkles. Examine visible scars; those that run across lymph vessels will obstruct lymph drainage. Look for pockets of edema and feel the tissues around the edematous areas, palpating for thickness, stiff tissue, or fibrotic tissue. Examine visible veins, looking for redness, swelling, heat, and pain. To assist in remembering the appearance of the skin before cellulite treatment, make notes on an outline of the figure, marking the location of scars, edema, moles, veins, and so on, and describing them.

STEP

BY

STEP

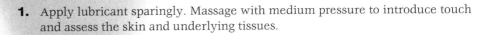

Conducting the Procedure

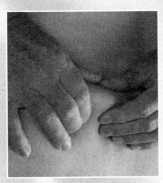

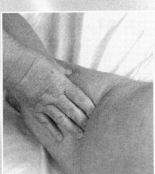

1. Apply lubricant sparingly. Massage with medium pressure to introduce touch and assess the skin and underlying tissues.

2. As the lubricant is absorbed, begin the connective tissue massage. Skin rolling is a good technique to reduce adhesions in the superficial fascia, the layer holding the fat cells. Pick up the skin between thumb and fingers. Roll it over the thumb in a continuous motion, beginning at the gluteal crease and working toward the waist. The fingers walk along, picking up tissue, and the thumbs follow, pushing through the tissue. Cover the entire gluteal region with skin rolling. Then use skin rolling on the posterior thigh, rolling from the knee to the gluteal crease. Repeat until the entire area is covered and the skin is flushed and warm. The purpose of this initial movement is to release the superficial fascia from underlying structures and improve its flexibility.

3. The purpose of the next stroke is to create a mesh of microtears in the superficial fascia, which will stretch and smooth the fascia. Press down into the skin with the tips of the fingers, the flat hand, a flat fist, or the lower arm in front of the elbow. Press into the skin very slowly until resistance is met. At that level begin sliding very slowly from the gluteal crease to the waist. Use lighter pressure over bony regions such as the iliac crest (the bony protuberance at the waist in the back). Repeat until the tissue in this area is warm, soft, and very pliable. The client should experience a burning sensation, but no intense pain. If the work is painful, use less pressure and move even more slowly.

4. Repeat the deep stroke on the posterior thigh, from the knee to the gluteal crease. Use lighter pressure over the soft area behind the knee and deeper pressure up the back of the thigh to the hip joint. Repeat until the entire posterior thigh has been worked.

5. Repeat steps one through four on the other leg.

6. Apply a cellulite cream if desired to the buttocks and thighs. Assist the client to turn over to a supine position. Drape warmly, but expose the hips and thighs.

7. Use skin rolling if possible on the anterior thigh. Some clients will not be able to tolerate it. Follow with the deep stroke from above the knee to the inguinal ligament. Use lighter pressure over the medial thigh. *Do not* perform the deep massage stroke over the femoral triangle where the lymph nodes and femoral nerve and artery are located. Repeat the deep massage stroke over the entire anterior thigh (except as cautioned above) until the thigh is warm, flushed, and supple.

8. Apply a cellulite cream if desired.

(continued)

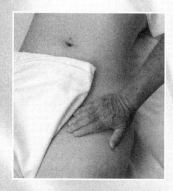

9. Begin LDM by massaging the inguinal lymph nodes with very slow, stationary circles, light pressure, for 2 to 3 minutes. Each circle should last 7 seconds.

10. Work the abdomen in a fan-shaped pattern. Place hands over abdomen between inguinal ligament and navel with the finger tips along the midline and the heels of the hands near the inguinal ligament. Using both hands, move the skin of the abdomen in large slow circles, seven circles lasting 7 seconds each, about 1 minute.

11. Move hands so that the fingertips are along the waist and the heels of the hands are close to the inguinal ligament, and massage as before for 1 minute.

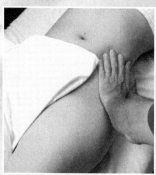

12. Move hands so that the fingertips reach down the side close to the massage table, between the waist and hip joint, with the heels of the hands near the inguinal ligament as before. Massage with slow circles, 7 seconds per circle, for 1 minute.

13. If necessary, repeat abdominal massage until there is a palpable change in the tissue.

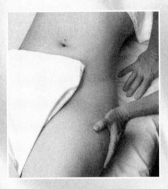

14. Massage along the "side seam" of the thigh. Place hands over the upper third of the iliotibial band, near the hip joint, and massage using slow, stationary circles for about 1 minute. Each circle should take 7 seconds, nearly 1 minute altogether.

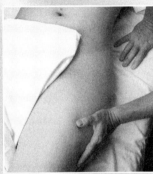

15. Place hands over the middle third of the iliotibial band, and massage using slow, stationary circles. Each circle should take 7 seconds, nearly 1 minute altogether.

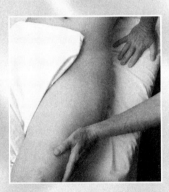

16. Place hands over the lower third of the iliotibial band, near the knee, and massage using slow, stationary circles. Each circle should take 7 seconds, nearly 1 minute altogether.

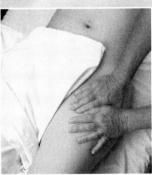

17. Place hands over the upper third of the thigh, inferior to the inguinal crease, covering the upper rectus femoris muscle, and massage using slow, stationary circles. Repeat circles seven times.

(continued)

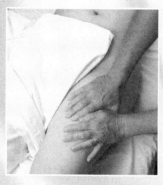

18. Place hands over the middle rectus femoris muscle area, and massage using stationary circles. Repeat circles seven times.

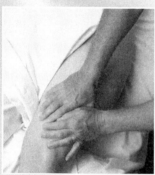

19. Place hands over the bottom of the rectus femoris muscle, superior to the knee, and massage using stationary circles. Repeat circles seven times.

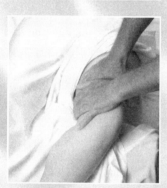

20. Roll the knee out slightly, away from the midline, to make access to the inner thigh easier. Place hands over the lower half of the medial thigh and massage using stationary circles. Repeat circles seven times.

21. Place hands around knee and use a scooping motion to move fluid toward the inguinal nodes. Each "scoop" should take 7 seconds, and should be repeated seven times. (A scoop is a semicircle.) Place one hand on each side of the knee, compress slightly, and stretch the skin in a semicircle toward the lymph nodes. Then release pressure and return to the point of origin.

22. Repeat the LDM strokes in reverse order, working from the knee to the inguinal crease.

23. Massage the inguinal nodes for 2 to 3 minutes.

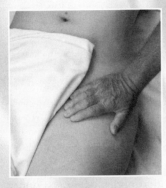

24. Using flat hands, massage the gluteal region in a fan-shaped pattern. Place hands so that the heels of the hands are close to the hip joint with fingers parallel to the gluteal crease. Massage using slow circles (each circle should last 7 seconds). Repeat 7 times.

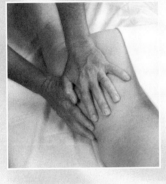

25. Place hands so that the heels of the hands are close to the hip joint with fingers pointing toward the sacrum and massage for 1 minute, using slow, stationary circles, 7 seconds each circle.

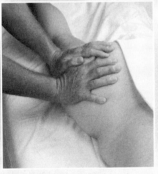

26. Place the hands so that the heels of the hands are close to the hip joint with fingers pointing toward the waist, parallel to the massage table. Massage for 1 minute as before.

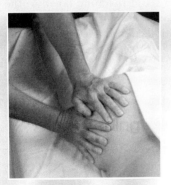

(continued)

27. Massage the lumbar region, using stationary circles repeated seven times.

28. Massage over the sacrum using stationary circles.

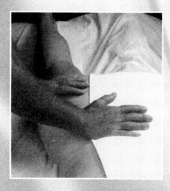

29. Massage over the back of the knee to open popliteal nodes using stationary circles. Repeat seven times.

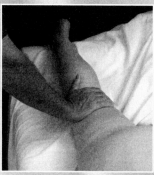

30. Place flat hands on the upper thigh, just below the gluteal crease. Massage for one minute with stationary circles. Repeat seven times.

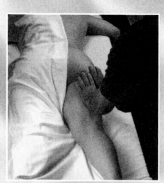

31. Place flat hands mid-thigh, with fingers of each hand reaching down to the massage table on each side. Massage for 1 minute, moving the skin in a semi-circle up toward the inguinal crease and out to the sides of the thigh. Repeat seven times, each scooping movement lasting about 7 seconds.

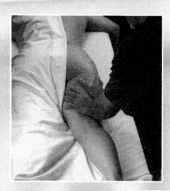

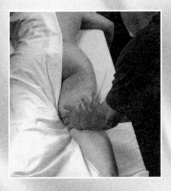

32. Place flat hands just above the knee on the lower thigh, with fingers reaching to the massage table on each side. Move the skin in a semicircle up toward the inguinal crease and out to the sides of the thigh, repeating the scooping movement seven times, 7 seconds each time.

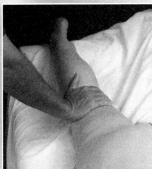

33. Massage the back of the knee, using stationary circles for 1 minute. Each circle should last 7 seconds.

34. Assist client to turn over into supine position. Drape warmly. Finish the lower quadrant by massaging over the inguinal nodes again, twenty circles.

35. Assist client to turn over into supine position. Drape warmly. Finish the lower quadrant by massaging over the inguinal nodes again, twenty circles.

The cellulite treatment can be followed with a body wrap. Remember that the total session including deep tissue massage, LDM and body wrap should not exceed an hour and a half. The body wrap is not recommended for anyone who is pregnant or who has high blood pressure.

At the end of the session, teach the client a stretch for anterior thigh, posterior thigh, and lateral thigh. Lunges, done correctly, are very effective. To stretch the lateral thigh, teach the client how to do side bends. Encourage the client to stretch daily, drink water, and eat fruits and vegetables.

Energetic and Mind-Body Effects of Lymph Drainage Massage

Lymph drainage massage has many beneficial effects and not just physiologic ones. Over the years, I have seen LDM affect clients on many levels. The deep relaxation LDM achieves in a conducive setting can lead client and therapist into nonordinary states of reality, much like meditative states. It is within such nonordinary states of reality that healing can arise, and for this mind-body work the success of the session depends on the setting, the energetic connection between the therapist and the client, and the work performed.

Establishing the Proper Setting

The setting must feel safe to both therapist and client. Privacy must be insured, and the room should be quiet, dim, and serene. Music, if used, should be unobtrusive. Outside noises should be muffled so they are distant and not distracting. The temperature must be comfortable, and the client and therapist must be able to relax.

For the client, the massage table should be comfortable, easy to climb onto, secure, and safe. Bolsters may be needed to ensure comfort, and the client must be warm.

For the therapist, body mechanics are essential. For long sessions on small areas of the body, like the face and neck, a sitting position is recommended. The height of the chair should be such that when the therapist sits back on the chair seat with the spine fully supported, the arms will rest comfortably on the table.

Massaging Appropriately

LDM is slow, light, repetitive, and rhythmical, which requires close attention. Proper LDM requires therapists to focus their attention very narrowly, counting the seconds and number of circles repetitively. To detect subtle changes in the soft tissue, the therapist must ignore distractions and focus attention only on the client. These subtle changes indicate that lymph fluid is moving in response to the work.

Such narrow focus, along with repetitive counting and relaxed breathing, often puts the therapist in a meditative state. Slow, repetitive massage movements, blending with the natural rhythms of the body, induce the same meditative state in the client. In this state, therapist and client can create an energetic bond. By stimulating lymph flow on a physiologic level, LDM can balance and harmonize the client's energy or biofield. This may explain why clients often report positive therapy outcomes that are not explained by the physiologic realities of the body and the massage. Apparently, inner work is done.

For example, clients may drift off and, in dreamlike states, begin to review their lives in their minds, reframing incidents and understanding themes that alter their perspectives. In this state, the clients may also experience visions, flashbacks, or regressive experiences. They may feel unpleasant familiar or unfamiliar emotions, and they might have such physical symptoms as pain from an old injury.

Preparing the Client

Obviously, inner experiences may be more than clients expect from massage. Although such experiences are beneficial, they are unsought and therefore may be unnerving. It is important, therefore, that therapists review the following guidelines:

- Clients can relax more completely when they trust their therapists. Trust builds as clients sense congruity in their therapists and feel that their therapists have integrity. A client's sense of congruity in a therapist depends on the client seeing or sensing that the therapist practices what he or she believes and is on a life path leading toward wholeness. Clients must feel sure that the therapist will never betray them or abuse their trust.

■ The therapist should recognize that the massage experience belongs to the client, not the therapist. The therapist should not take emotional outbursts personally nor become involved. For example, the therapist should offer no advice about the client's personal experiences or problems.

■ If the client is distressed and upset, the therapist should remain calm and reassuring and offer a tissue if there are any tears. Sometimes, the relaxed dream state is so real that clients are unsure where they are or what is happening. If this happens, the therapist should reassure the clients and let the clients know they are safe.

■ Allow clients to explore the meanings of inner experiences. Do not interpret. Instead, turn the clients back to their histories for understanding. It can be very tempting to try to explain an experience to a client, but it does not help, because it short-circuits growth. Like dreams, a client's inner experiences during a body-mind session often contain universally recognized symbols. However, the symbol's real meaning for the client will be very individual. For instance, some clients may interpret the sensation of weightlessness as flying and they will feel free and exhilarated; others may interpret weightlessness as being disconnected and unstable and possibly frightening. Rather than attempting to explain the experience, let the client know that many people have similar experiences in similar settings. It is all right for therapists to tell a story, perhaps about their experiences receiving massage, and to show how the experiences helped the therapist understand themselves better.

■ Do not invalidate an experience for a client by withdrawing or disapproving. This may be difficult if, say, the client experiences a past life and the therapist does not believe in past lives. Stay detached, focus on the LDM, and allow the client to realize the internal experience fully. If the client relates an extreme experience, such as an out-of-body experience or an alien abduction, the therapist should remain neutral and uninvolved. The therapist's job is to massage, not to counsel clients about their inner experiences. If the client wants the therapist to respond to his or her experience, the therapist should say that they lack the understanding or skills to deal with the experience and should refer the client to someone who is qualified to discuss the matter.

■ It is important that therapists stay in touch with their own processes and reactions to clients' experiences. Client memories, emotions, and experiences can trigger possibly uncomfortable reactions in therapists, especially if the experiences synchronize with their experiences. Therapists may empathize, but they must keep their feelings separate from clients' feelings. The session must focus on the client. If the client has experiences that bring up uncomfortable memories for the therapist, the therapist should not discuss those feelings with the client. The therapist should seek counseling at another time, with another therapist.

■ Make sure clients are oriented and can drive safely before they leave. If clients have entered nonordinary states of reality, they will need time to return to full alertness. Physical reactions may be slower than usual, and clients may not be entirely aware of everything in the environment when leaving the table. Offer clients water, check their clothes to ensure they have buttoned things correctly, and walk with them until they are fully alert and able to drive safely.

Enjoying the Results

One of the results of this kind of meditative work is that therapists as well as clients will experience meditative effects. Therapists who are regularly performing meditative massage techniques may experience increased intuitive response to situations, periodic flashes of childhood trauma, turning away from some of the coarser demands of life, offending significant others by one's growth and change, wanting diet changes, and so on. Therapists who are not ready for the life changes resulting from meditative practice may find themselves resistant to the discipline demanded by this kind of work: the slow, measured pace and the focus and mindfulness necessary for effective therapy. Simple breathing exercises, as well as learning how to relax and slow down, will help.

Like their clients, estheticians or massage therapists may feel they are getting more than they bargained for when clients react to the work on many levels. When therapists are unprepared for this possibility, it can be overwhelming. The following information from Robert Leichtman, M.D., may help therapists understand the reciprocal energetic effect of meditative body work. In a letter to Judy Dean, quoted with permission, Dr. Leichtman gave the following explanation of the energetic exchange that occurs in massage:

> There are other even more subtle things going on when there is a therapeutic interaction between the client and the care giver (of any type). Depending (a great amount) on the consciousness of the healer, the client is drawn into the aura (energy field) of the healer (person doing the massage, etc.) This is akin to a mother holding an infant, bathing the child in her affection and expectations. This sort of energetic radiation fills the energy field of the child or client. Usually, this will be a healthy experience unless, that is, that the person doing the treatment is full of conflict, anxiety or some other dark mood. . . .

Now if the healer is in a higher, meditative state of mind, this higher level of awareness is also transmitted to the client. That is, just as a mother can draw a fussing infant into her maternal peace and quiet love of life thereby soothing the infant, so also a healer can draw the client into a more tranquil, meditative, contemplative state of mind. This can be a state of mind in which they can begin to register subtle insights and experience the state of goodwill in which forgiveness, tolerance and letting go, can occur.

As you undoubtedly know, the person who is loaded down with lots of unresolved conflict and gobs of retained fear, anger, doubt, guilt, grief, etc. will just retain it forever. The more tense, angry, full of self-pity, etc., we are, the more we keep the lid on these dark moods as well as add to them by the tendency to nurse grievances. They are released only as we cultivate a deeply relaxed state in which we can float in a quiet, contemplative state where the far more subtle healing forces of goodwill and self-respect and wisdom can function. These are the healing states in which we can let go of anger, fear, guilt, and can allow healing insights to come to us.

My point is, the higher state of wisdom, love, joy, and inclusive acceptance of the healer becomes a catalyst and stimulus for the client to reach a similar state. It is not just relaxation (or lymph flow). This higher state of consciousness is where psychological healing (as well as physical healing) can occur.[44]

More information on body-mind experiences in massage and other therapies can be found in *The Ethics of Caring* (Taylor, K. [1995]. Hanford Mead Publishers).

CHAPTER 15

Using Lymph Drainage Massage with Other Treatments

Lymph drainage massage can be easily and effectively combined with other techniques, including:

- cellulite therapy, to speed the removal of toxins and reduce edema and inflammation.
- sports massage, to speed the healing of injuries and reduce inflammation and edema.
- deep-tissue massage, to reduce postsession soreness and swelling.
- facials, to enhance the skin from the inside and outside.
- body-mind work, to produce a deeply relaxed state for inner work.
- detoxifying treatments, to speed the removal of cellular waste.

Working with Cellulite Therapy

LDM is an important part of cellulite therapy. LDM helps to remove cellular waste and toxins, reduce inflammation, reduce edema, and improve the skin condition. Cellulite massage is discussed in detail in Chapter 13.

Conducting Sports Massage for Soft-Tissue Injuries

LDM very effectively reduces swelling and speeds healing. Using it for acute conditions, however, is the prerogative of advanced practitioners. LDM for soft-tissue injuries can be undertaken safely only when basic principles and movements have been mastered and the therapist has clocked many hours of LDM. The instructions that follow presuppose knowledge of the basics.

To avoid complicating an injury or acute condition, therapists must consider the following before performing LDM on a person who has been injured recently, who is postoperative, or whose condition may be considered acute.

- Before any LDM is undertaken, the client must have obtained medical attention to rule out broken bones, torn ligaments or muscles, and any other massage contraindications.

- Open wounds, surgeries, and the like must heal before tissues are touched by a massage therapist. Postsurgical work must not be undertaken until enough time has elapsed for healing. The best way to ensure this is to insist on a prescription for LDM from the client's physician as long as the client is still under the physician's care. This request is usually honored, and working to the prescription provides direction and perspective. Once clients have been released by their physicians and need no more follow-up visits, massage may be assumed safe.

- Infection, if any, must have healed, as it is a serious LDM contraindication.

- When the client can clearly sustain an LDM session, use it to reduce swelling and speed healing. The principle is to drain the appropriate lymph nodes first, then work on the injured area. Drain abdominal or lower limb edema into the inguinal lymph nodes; drain trunk and upper extremities edema into the axillary lymph nodes. Be aware that the greater the edema, the longer it will take to reduce. This requires more repetitions of the massage strokes, possibly as many as 100 repetitions in each area.

- When the preceding precautions have been observed, LDM may be safely performed daily. When progress is maintained for 24 hours, give sessions every other day or every third day. As the condition improves, gradually lengthen the time between sessions. If the client cannot have daily sessions, instruct the client to self-treat.

Reducing Fibrosis and Scar Tissue

When an injury or a surgery has healed, the client's readiness for other work can be assessed by considering whether the client reports the pain has greatly decreased or disappeared, the wound or surgery has obviously healed and swelling has reduced, and no infection (local or general) is present.

The next step, if muscle contracture is present and the client is emotionally ready, is to reduce fibrosis and scar tissue. Following that, muscles must be retrained to balance movement. Deep-tissue massage to relieve muscle contracture or to open fascia may be undertaken. Deep-tissue massage can soften contractures and reduce keloid ridges. It also breaks down and even inhibits adhesions. Additionally, it is wise to stretch muscles that are being worked to increase range of motion.

Because one side effect of deep-tissue massage is inflammation, follow deep-tissue activities with LDM to reduce that inflammation and prevent additional swelling. Use friction strokes across the fibers and along the length of the fibers of scars and keloid ridges. Follow with LDM to reduce inflammation.

Engage the client in the healing process by encouraging home follow-up. In injury rehabilitation work, it is important to guide the client in stretching exercises that relax and retrain affected muscles. Strengthening exercises may also be needed as muscles may have become weak while healing.

Encourage clients to seek movement training to prevent new injuries and to restore muscle balance. For example, clients who are athletes should have some training from coaches. Others, like those learning yoga or tai chi, benefit from other, similar movement training as a way to increase wellness. Encourage clients to participate in these activities.

Pairing with Deep-Tissue Massage

LDM can be used effectively with deep-tissue massage to reduce postsession soreness and swelling. Deep-tissue massage focuses on connective tissue, using specific strokes to change posture and movement and reduce scar tissue and chronic muscle contracture. Deep-tissue massage movements elongate and relax muscles by creating microtears in the connective tissue of the muscle. Deep-tissue massage is often combined with stretching or other movement training to ensure that the muscle remains relaxed and stretched while healing. Deep-tissue massage produces inflammation as a side effect.

Following deep-tissue massage with LDM reduces inflammation, speeds healing of microtears, and helps new scar tissue in the muscle form correctly.

Complementing Skin Care

LDM, originally developed in France as a part of the beauty industry, is an important part of skin care. LDM improves the skin's appearance and texture, reducing the fibrosis and damage resulting from exposure to cold and sun. LDM also improves circulation, bringing in nutrition for skin cells and removing cellular waste and disease-causing micro-organisms.

Engaging with Body-Mind Therapies

LDM is ideal for body-mind therapies because it is gentle, extremely relaxing, and, in the right circumstances, trance inducing. LDM's very slow pace and regular rhythm help to induce a state of nonordinary consciousness in which clients can do internal work. More information about the body-mind effects of LDM is included in Chapter 14.

Amplifying Detoxifying Treatments

LDM is useful when clients are undergoing detoxifying treatments, like body wraps, fasting, and purifying diets. However, therapists should be aware that combining therapies such as wraps or fasting with LDM can trigger healing crises. The combination can make the client feel ill with flulike symptoms, for example. Body wraps work by creating an artificial fever, increasing body heat, with the same effects on the body as a genuine fever in response to pathogens. If the therapist feels that a client may react to the combination of treatments with a healing crisis, it is better not to combine the therapies but to offer the treatments as separate sessions on different days. If a client is responding to fasting with symptoms of illness, wait to offer LDM until the client is no longer fasting. It will still be effective in helping the immune system to remove cellular waste and disease-causing organisms.

CHAPTER 16

Self-Massage Using Lymph Drainage Massage Techniques

*N*urses, estheticians and massage therapists, and other similar caregivers are as much educators as they are therapists and technicians. Teaching clients to understand the purpose and effects of the therapy is always beneficial and encourages compliance. This is especially true with LDM. Teaching one's clients to self-treat is valuable for several reasons. First, many clients cannot afford daily LDM sessions, but progress is more significant with daily therapy. Teaching clients to self-treat daily with weekly professional sessions yields better results than if the clients simply come in once a week for LDM sessions with professionals.

Besides self-treatment for lymphedema, clients may want to self-massage for beauty and health reasons. Daily lymph massage of the face and neck helps to maintain the skin in the best possible condition. Massaging the tissues of the face and neck, especially the lymph nodes, when the client feels a cold or another minor illness coming on helps to stimulate lymph circulation and the circulation of immune cells in the lymph vessels and nodes. Clients who suffer chronic sinus infections and nasal allergies will find LDM of the face very comforting.

People whose work demands that they stand all day, and who suffer edema and painful legs and feet as a result, will find that daily LDM helps to reduce edema, improve circulation, and reduce or eliminate leg pain. Obese patients who suffer from edema, especially in the lower extremities, will find that daily self-massage reduces the edema, improves circulation, reduces pain, and helps to prevent pathological changes to the skin that are common in chronic edema.

Women who suffer hormone-related bloating and breast swelling and tenderness will find that regular LDM helps to eliminate each of these symptoms. Daily breast massage is important for breast health. Besides increasing lymph circulation and keeping breast tissues healthy, women who massage their breasts regularly will become very familiar with the way their breasts feel and will be able to detect subtle changes in breast tissue more quickly than with monthly breast self-examinations.

Knowing LDM basics enables family members to help each other with pain, edema, and scar tissue following soft-tissue injuries. Many painful soft-tissue problems, such as muscle tension, muscle spasm, inflammation, and overuse injuries, respond to LDM.

Teamwork on the part of the therapist or esthetician and the client produces the best results. It is a good idea to teach clients to self-treat so they can continue treatment between appointments with professional therapists. Routine self-massage helps to maintain the progress obtained in the professional session and allows the therapist to make greater progress during each session.

It is important for clients to understand the contraindications and appropriate use of LDM. When teaching clients simple techniques for self-massage, therapists should also make sure that clients understand when *not* to perform LDM.

Therapists can demonstrate simple procedures and help clients practice movements, then in the next session discuss the client's experience with self-massage and refine the client's skill.

Self-Massaging the Face and Neck

Self-massage of the face and neck can be performed while sitting or lying. Probably the best position is seated with the back, neck, and head supported. The client is less likely to fall asleep while self-massaging while seated.

The basic principles for self-massage are the same as for professional massage therapists and estheticians. Using light pressure ($\frac{1}{2}$ to 8 ounces per square inch), move the skin in a circular or semicircular direction, repeating the moves regularly and slowly, six to ten repetitions a minute, and move lymph toward the lymph nodes.

Because the massage of the head and neck takes half an hour or more, some might find it easier to do the massage in sections, massaging the neck one day and the face the next. The work can be done with or without lotion or cream; it is a matter of taste. Heat stimulates lymph circulation, so steaming the face and neck first with a hot, moist towel is a good idea. Allow the moist, hot towel to cool to room temperature while massaging the face lightly through the towel.

Focusing on the Neck

1. Seated comfortably, begin with the lymph nodes. Place the hands above the clavicle, next to the sternocleidomastoid muscles. Massage this area for 2 to 3 minutes using stationary circles, about 7 per minute. It helps to have a loudly ticking clock nearby to count the seconds to make sure the massage movements are consistent. Stationary circles should last 6 to 10 seconds, which is very slow. The natural tendency is to move faster unless one is watching a clock.

2. Next, massage the lymph nodes below and behind the ear for 2 to 3 minutes using stationary circles, about 7 per minute.

3. Massage the anterior cervical chain of the nodes. Place flat fingers over the sternocleidomastoid muscles on either side of the neck, spreading the fingers to cover the muscles from the ear to the medial ends of the clavicle at the bottom of the throat. Massage lightly for at least 1 minute. Then, place flat fingers on the sides of the neck between the ear and the top of the shoulder, and massage lightly for another minute, about seven circles.

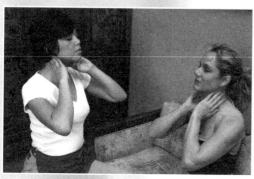

4. Cover the back of the neck, from the hairline to the collar, with flat fingers and massage the back of the neck for 1 minute, seven circles for about 7 seconds each.

5. Place the fingertips under the jawline from the chin to the ear, and massage the submandibular nodes lightly with 7 circles, each about 7 seconds.

6. Finish the neck massage by brushing the back of the neck lightly from the spine toward the front of the neck for about 1 minute. Brush the front of the neck lightly from the ear and jawline down to the clavicle.

Targeting the Face

1. Place flat fingers and the palm over the angle of the jaw. Massage over the lymph nodes for 2 to 3 minutes using stationary circles, about 7 per minute.

2. Massage the chin with flat fingertips for about 1 minute. Use seven circles per minute, watching a clock to maintain consistent speed.

3. Then, using all fingertips, massage just above the jawline from the corners of the mouth to the angle of the jaw, for about 1 minute.

4. Then, massage the upper lip using one or two fingers of each hand, for about 1 minute.

5. Use one or two fingers of each hand to massage the nose for 1 minute, about seven circles.

6. Place fingertips in a curve from the inner corners of the eye to the corners of the mouth. Massage for at least 1 minute.

7. Finally, brush lightly from the nose down to the angle of the jaw for about 1 minute, then from the chin out to the angle of the jaw for about 1 minute.

8. Place the fingers in front of the ears over the preauricular joints. Massage the preauricular nodes for 2 to 3 minutes.

(continued)

9. Place the palms of the hands on the forehead and the fingers on the scalp and massage this area with large stationary circles for about 1 minute, about seven circles per minute.

10. Then, place the palms on the temple between the eyes and ears with the fingers on the scalp, and massage for about 1 minute, in seven circles.

11. Next, place the palms of the hands behind the ears with the fingers covering the back of the head and massage the scalp for 1 minute, seven circles about 7 seconds each.

12. Place fingers of both hands along the base of the skull and massage for about 1 minute, seven circles about 7 seconds each.

13. Massage the lymph nodes behind and below the ears for 2 or 3 minutes.

14. Massage the anterior cervical chain of nodes along the sternocleidomastoid muscle for 2 or 3 minutes.

15. Massage the posterior cervical chain of nodes along the sides of the neck between the ear and the shoulder for 2 or 3 minutes.

16. Massage the lymph nodes above the clavicle for 2 or 3 minutes. Finish by lightly brushing the entire face and neck from the top to the bottom.

STEP

BY

*S*elf-Massaging the Upper Limbs

STEP

1. For this massage, it is probably most comfortable to lie down, propped by a couple of pillows. Raise the arm overhead, supported by a pillow. Place the fingers of the opposite hand deep into the center of the armpit and massage lightly for 2 or 3 minutes. Move the skin in stationary circles, about seven circles per minute, which is very slow.

2. Next, place the flat fingers just above the armpit on the arm and massage for 2 or 3 minutes, using stationary circles.

3. Reach under the pectoralis muscle in front of the armpit and massage for 2 or 3 minutes.

4. Reach under the latissimus dorsi muscle at the back of the armpit and massage the lymph nodes there for 2 or 3 minutes.

5. Massage the chest wall around the outside of the breast. Place one hand above the breast and below the clavicle and massage for about 1 minute, using stationary circles, about seven circles per minute.

6. Place the entire hand next to the outside of the breast and massage for 1 minute, using stationary circles.

7. Place the entire hand on the rib cage under the breast and massage for 1 minute.

8. Place the fingertips of both hands on the sternum and massage for 1 minute.

(continued)

9. Massage the breast. Divide the breast into four sections and massage each section for about 1 minute, using stationary circles and repeating the circles seven times in a minute. Finish this section by brushing from the sternum over and around the breast toward the lymph nodes in the armpit.

10. Massage the upper arm. Lightly and very slowly brush the lymph toward the lymph nodes from the elbow to the shoulder joint. Repeat each brush stroke seven or more times before moving to a new area on the upper arm.

11. Massage the lower arm. Lightly and very slowly brush the lymph toward the upper arm from the wrist toward the elbow. Repeat each brush stroke seven or more times before moving to a new area of the lower arm.

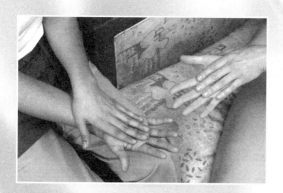

12. Massage the hand. Use the fingertips of one hand to massage the pads in the palm of the other hand, using stationary circles, about 1 minute. Wrap the fingers of the opposite hand around one of the fingers on the hand to be massaged, with the thumb on the section of the finger closest to the palm. Massage each finger for about 1 minute, using stationary circles, about seven circles per minute.

13. Repeat the brush strokes slowly from the hand to the shoulder. Finish by massaging the lymph nodes in the axilla again.

Self-Massaging the Lower Limbs

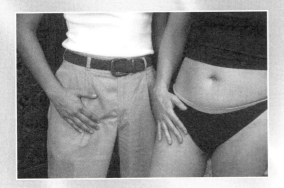

1. Self-massage of the lower limbs can be a little awkward, especially if one lacks flexibility. However, it can still be very effective and should be attempted. To massage the inguinal nodes, lie down on a bed, face up, upper body supported by one or two pillows. Rest one hand gently over the top of the thigh, just below the inguinal ligament. Without pressing deeply into the tissue, try to locate the femoral pulse. Then, using the pulse as another landmark, place one hand along the inguinal ligament with the fingers reaching to the area where the femoral pulse was located.

   Using light pressure, move the skin around in a slow circle, taking about 7 seconds to complete the circle. Repeat the circles for 2 to 3 minutes until there is a palpable change in the tissue. Moving in larger circles, the skin should feel softer, warmer, and more elastic.

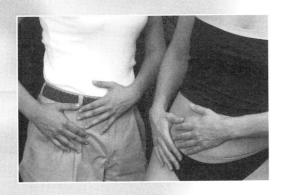

2. Place two hands on the abdomen, between the inguinal ligament and the navel. Using both hands, move the skin of the abdomen in large circles, taking about 7 seconds to complete a circle. Massage this area for 2 to 3 minutes. If the abdomen is large or the hands small, it might be necessary to massage the abdomen in sections. Cover the area from the midline to the side seam, from the waist to the inguinal ligament, massaging each area at least 1 minute.

(continued)

3. To massage the leg, sit up enough to reach the entire thigh, placing pillows to support the back and elevate the knee with a small pillow. Place two hands on the upper thigh, near the inguinal ligament, covering the top and outside of the thigh. Move the skin in as large circles as possible, very slowly. Take about 7 seconds to complete one circle, and repeat for at least 1 minute. Move down the thigh a hand's width and repeat. Work down the thigh to the knee.

4. Bend the knee more so that the back of the thigh is accessible. Placing the hands behind the thigh, move the skin in circles, taking about 7 seconds to complete a circle. Repeat for at least 1 minute. Move the hands to another location on the back of the thigh, until the whole area has been massaged. Grasp both sides of the knee lightly and massage the area for at least 1 minute.

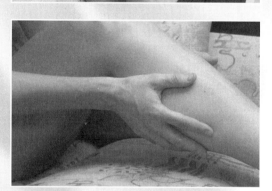

5. Remove the small pillow supporting the knee and extend the leg flat on the bed. Bending over to reach the lower leg, place both hands below the knee, wrapping around as much of the lower leg as possible. Move the skin in large, slow circles as before, taking at least 1 minute. Move down the leg in small increments, working at least 1 minute on each area.

6. Covering the ankles with flat fingers, move the skin in slow circles for 1 minute. Massage the top of the foot with one hand, using slow circles, for about 1 minute. Massage the bottom of the foot in two steps: the ball of the foot, then the heel pad. It is more difficult to move the skin on the sole of the foot, and it is tempting to use heavier pressure. Continue to use light pressure, about 1 ounce, and move the skin as well as possible in slow circles for about 1 minute.

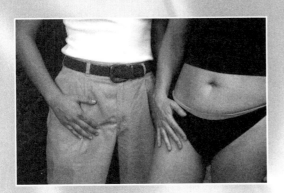

7. Slide the hands slowly from the foot to the knee, repeating seven times in 1 minute. Repeat on the back of the lower leg, sliding slowly from the heel to the knee seven times, very slowly with light pressure. Slide one or both hands from the knee to the hip, using light pressure, moving very slowly and repeating at least seven times.

8. Massage the inguinal lymph nodes again for 2 or 3 minutes.

Treating Soft-Tissue Injuries

For recent injuries that have begun to heal but are still swollen and painful, LDM is beneficial. First, make sure that the injury is examined to rule out underlying serious injuries, unless the injury is minor and has begun to heal, and pain is reduced. Do not massage over areas with open cuts, scratches, abrasions, or surgical incisions. Wait until these areas have healed to avoid infection.

Palpate the injured area and locate the outer edge of the painful area. Before moving to another area on the perimeter of the injury, beginning at the outer edge of the injured area, use the fingers to make small, slow circles, about 7 seconds per circle and repeating for at least 1 minute or until there is a palpable change in the tissue. Work in a circle around the edge of the injured area. Work in a spiral gradually toward the most painful area in the center. If the injury is very tender, this can take a long time. At the end of the session, pain should be reduced and bruising less visible.

If the injury is old and completely healed but still swollen, even if it is years old, a combination of connective-tissue massage and LDM can help. Scars are not necessarily visible; inflammation in the skin and muscles can result in scarring that can be felt although it cannot be seen. To reduce scar tissue, first stretch the connective tissue. Use skin rolling, cross-fiber friction, or deep, slow strokes until the area is red and warm. Connective-tissue massage should not be painful, but there will be a burning sensation when done correctly. Skin rolling is performed by picking up the skin between thumb and fingers and rolling the skin over the fingers with the thumb. Alternate hands so the movement is continuous along the tissue. Cross-fiber friction is performed by rubbing across or at right angles to scar tissue until a burning sensation is felt. To perform the deep, slow massage stroke that stretches the superficial fascia, press stiff fingers into the skin, then push slowly along the length of the scarred area with enough pressure to feel a burn in the tissues. Follow with LDM as described previously.

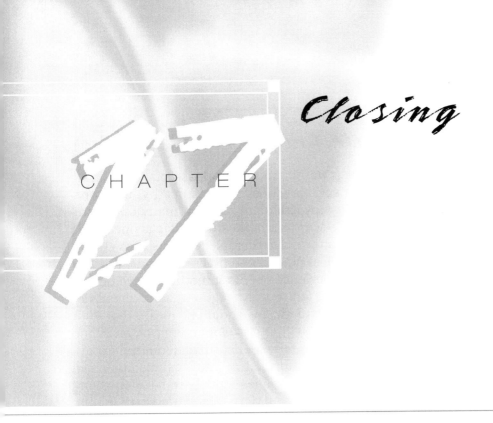

Closing

CHAPTER 17

*A*lthough the concept of a healing crisis is not generally recognized outside alternative therapies, massage therapists and others in similar fields have experienced this phenomenon in their practices. Clients who begin health regimens that depart from their lifestyles may experience difficult periods. They may reexperience symptoms of previous illnesses, such as childhood asthma. They may report that they taste antibiotics, although they have taken none in years. They may start to ache in the area of an old injury. These experiences are temporary, but they can be alarming if the therapist does not prepare the client for the experience.

Responding to the Health Crisis

A health crisis can happen to clients who are receiving one or a series of LDMs. Therapists should tell clients that occasionally people feel flulike or other symptoms after massage. Instruct the clients to drink fluids, rest, and in general treat themselves as if they have the flu. A healing crisis is temporary and is accepted among alternative practitioners as a sign therapy is working. If the symptoms last longer than a day or two, the client may actually be ill and should seek treatment.

Understanding the Health Crisis

The concept of a healing crisis is purely nonmedical, associated with the empiric tradition that includes such practices as homeopathy, naturopathy, body work and massage therapy, iridology, and, in many cases, chiropractic and osteopathy. The concept of the healing crisis is one of the underlying principles unique to alternative therapies that set those therapies apart from mainstream medical practice. In practical terms, the idea of a healing crisis refers to the experience clients sometimes have of feeling worse before they feel better, when they begin to adopt healthier lifestyles. Massage therapists and estheticians should be aware that their clients will sometimes experience healing crises following LDM. When they have been informed, clients generally feel positive about the experiences. Clients who have not been informed of the healing crisis can become alarmed and feel that their therapies somehow harmed them. Therefore, communication is crucial, but it is also important not to overemphasize the possibility of a healing crisis, because it does not happen to everyone.

The concept of a healing crisis derives from the belief that disease, particularly chronic disease, is caused by toxicity and that toxicity is the result of occurrences accumulated in the human system over time. A healing crisis results from physical and emotional pollution, and the symptoms the client experiences during the healing crisis can be both physical and emotional. Clients who are educated by their therapists as to the possibility of a healing crisis generally view the experience as a positive sign that the therapy is beneficial.

At the physical level, toxicity is believed to be caused by years of inadequate diet that has polluted the system. It is also attributed to continual suppression of acute disease, through the overuse of pain medicine, antibiotics, and the like, which appears to build toxicity in the system.

Although the concept of the healing crisis arose in response to awareness of physical pollutants, massage therapists, body workers, and estheticians have long been aware that suppressed emotions are also pollutants to the **soma** and that skilled touch readily activates both physical and nonphysical symptoms that can alarm the client.

Accepting the Health Crisis

Healing crises are to be taken in stride. Generally, clients enjoy LDM and afterward feel better, relaxed, and soothed. A healing crisis will not occur with every client or with every massage session. When a healing crisis does occur, it can begin spontaneously during the LDM session or it can be precipitated by the work and occur later. The reaction may be physical (e.g., flu symptoms, shivering, mild nausea) or nonphysical (e.g., weeping, emotional release, visions). The healing crisis might involve releases on more than one level. For instance, the client may weep during the massage, remembering a childhood sorrow, then go home and suffer upper respiratory symptoms. When this kind of event occurs during a session, experienced practitioners realize that their responsibility is to remain with the client, quietly and sensitively, until the release is over.

With experience, practitioners will come to recognize clients who have greater potential for healing crises than others. Some clients are emotionally too unstable to weather the fallout of some treatments. Other clients may have simply neglected their health for so many years that a healing crisis is inevitable when they begin to change their lives, including receiving massage treatments. When in doubt, limit the length and frequency of lymph massage. Combine LDM with other massage techniques that are more generalized. Also, be prepared to refer clients to appropriate counselors or medical practitioners if they are having difficulty with memories or feelings experienced during or after the massage, or are feeling ill for more than a day or two after the session.

Glossary

Acquired immunity Ability to resist disease acquired through exposure to an infectious agent.

Active immunity Development of antibodies due to exposure to disease-causing agents, either through direct exposure or vaccination.

Afferent vessels Lymphatic vessels leading into lymph nodes; *see also efferent vessels.*

Aggregated lymph nodules Clusters of lymph tissue in the intestine and appendix that respond to antigens (disease-causing agents) in the intestine; also called Peyer's patches.

Antibodies Protein molecules created by the body in response to antigens (disease-causing agents); destroy antigens.

Antigens Disease-causing substances.

Autoimmune diseases Condition in which the immune system attacks the body's own tissues and the immune system fails to recognize self-cells and attacks them as if they were invaders.

Basement membrane Layer of connective tissue that surrounds organs and vessels, providing support.

Basophil Type of lymph cell involved in allergic reactions and inflammation.

B-cells Lymph cells that produce antibodies.

Chyle Digested dietary fat.

Cisterna chyli Reservoir at the lower end of the thoracic duct that receives chyle from the intestines via lacteals.

Edema Condition in which excess interstitial fluid saturates the tissues causing swelling.

Efferent vessels Vessels leading out of lymph nodes, carrying lymph fluid toward the largest vessels, the lymph ducts.

Elephantiasis Scarring of lymphatic vessels and/or nodes that causes obstruction of lymph flow resulting in an enlarged limb (usually the leg and genital region); caused by filariasis.

Endothelial cells Layer of endothelial cells make up the walls of blood and lymph vessels.

Erythrocytes Mature red blood cells.

Flap valves Loosely overlapping cells that form the walls of the lymph capillaries; attached to surrounding structures with fibers that cause the capillaries to stretch and relax, which causes the flap valves to separate and allow fluid to enter the lymph capillaries.

Immune system Lymph cells, tissues, and organs and their functions.

Inflammation Defensive reaction involving cells and chemicals in response to injury or in response to a physical, chemical, or biological agent that damages cells.

Interstitia Spaces between tissue cells.

Interstitial fluid Filtrate from blood vessels that bathes and nourishes tissue cells.

Lacteals Specialized lymphatic vessels in the intestine that convey chyle (digested fat) to the cisterna chyli.

Leukocytes White blood or scavenger cells that attack foreign cells and foreign matter in the tissues and bloodstream.

Lymph Clear or yellowish fluid that is absorbed from body tissues into the lymphatic system, where it passes through lymph nodes before being returned to blood circulation; contains white blood cells, a few red blood cells, proteins, microorganisms, and microscopic particles.

Lymphatic ducts The two largest lymph vessels, the right lymphatic duct or the thoracic duct.

Lymphatic pump Spontaneous contraction of the smooth muscle cells in the walls of lymph vessels, which has the effect of propelling lymph.

Lymphangions Muscular segments of lymph vessels with bicuspid valves at each end to prevent lymph backflow.

Lymphatics Pertaining to lymph; also used to refer to lymph vessels.

Lymphatic system Consists of lymph, lymph tissue, lymph vessels, nodes, ducts, spleen, thymus, and tonsils; moves fluid out of tissue spaces into lymph vessels, where it is filtered by lymph nodes before returning to the blood circulatory system.

Lymphatic tissue A network of fibers and cells that contain lymphocytes; also called lymphoid tissue, includes lymph vessels and organs.

Lymph capillaries Smallest vessels in the lymphatic system; arise in the tissues and absorb fluid from the tissues; very porous, little or no basement membrane, consist of one layer of endothelial cells.

Lymph drainage massage (LDM) A gentle, rhythmic style of massage that mimics the action of the lymphatic system using precise rhythm and pressure to reduce edema.

Lymphedema Chronic swelling that results from venous or lymphatic vessel malformation, also called congenital or primary lymphedema, or from obstruction of lymph vessels and/or nodes, also called obstructive or secondary lymphedema.

Lymphedema disease A chronic progressive swelling of soft tissue with pathological changes to tissue. *See also primary lymphedema and secondary lymphedema.*

Lymph nodes Small (1–25 mm in diameter), bean-shaped masses of lymph tissue located along the pathways of lymphatic vessels: consist of fibrous coverings containing lymph cells and fibers arranged into sinuses; usually have small depressions on one side called the hila, where efferent vessels emerge from the node; afferent vessels attach to the lymph node at various points around the periphery of the node.

Lymph nodules A collecton of lymph tissue in the mucus tissue lining the respiratory and digestive tracts.

Lymphocytes White blood cells formed in lymphatic tissue (lymph nodes, spleen, thymus, tonsils, Peyer patches, and bone marrow); divided into T- and B-cells and natural killer (NK) cells.

Lymphoid Resembling or referring to lymph tissue or the lymphatic system.

Lymph vessels Vessels larger than lymph capillaries; the channels through which lymph flows.

Macrophages White blood cells that digest foreign cells and foreign material in the bloodstream and tissues, also called phagocytes.

Monocytes Immature macrophages that digest foreign cells and foreign material in the bloodstream and tissues.

Natural killer (NK) cells Like B- or T-cells, leukocytes that destroy virus-infected cells.

Neutrophils Type of white blood cells, phagocytes.

Nonspecific immunity Immunity that depends on various structures and activities in the body reacting to all invading cells in the same way, without memory for specific antigens or the creation of antibodies.

Passive immunity Resistance to disease acquired through the transfer of antibodies from another person, usually from mother to fetus.

Phagocytes Cells that destroy microorganisms by engulfing them.

Phagocytized Foreign cells destroyed and particles absorbed through the membranes of white blood cells by phagocytes.

Precollectors Larger lymph vessels that carry lymph away from tissues and toward lymph nodes.

Primary lymphedema A disease process due to congenital malformation of blood and/or lymph vessels.

Right lymphatic duct One of the two largest lymph vessels; receives lymph fluid from the right arm and right side of the upper trunk, and the right side of the neck and head, then delivers the fluid to the right subclavian vein.

Secondary lymphedema A disease caused by obstruction of lymph vessels due to infection, injury, irradiation, or surgery.

Soma The body of an organism.

Specific immunity Immunity resulting from the creation of antibodies that remember and destroy microorganisms after first exposure.

Spleen Lymph organ that stores blood and produces lymphocytes and monocytes; located along blood vessels rather than lymph vessels; considered the "lymph node of the blood."

Stationary circle Using flat fingers, gently contact the skin, compress slightly, and stretch the tissue with a circular movement toward the lymph nodes.

T-cells Lymphocytes that attacks foreign cells; differentiated into helper T-cells, suppressor T-cells, and natural killer (NK) T-cells.

Thoracic duct Largest lymph vessel; drains fluid from the lower body, viscera, upper left trunk and arm, and left side of the head and neck; empties into the left subclavian vein.

Thymus Endocrine gland consisting of connective tissue and lymph tissue; produces a hormone that helps T-cells mature; helps with newborn immunity.

Tonsils Lymph nodes located around the opening to the respiratory and digestive tracts; destroy foreign cells and particles that enter those tracts; includes pharyngeal, palatine, and lingual tonsils.

Venous angle Junction of the internal, external, and anterior jugular veins and the subclavian vein with the thoracic duct on the left side, or the right lymphatic duct on the right side; near the superior end of the sternum.

Resources

American Society of Lymphology
P.O. Box 14853
Lenexa, KS 66285-4853
e-Mail: info@lymphology.com
URL: http://www.lymphology.com

Associated Bodyworkers and Massage Professionals
Referrals for massage therapists
URL: http://www.abmp.com

Desert Resorts School of Somatherapy
2100 N. Palm Canyon, Bldg. C
Palm Springs, CA 92262
Classes and therapy available
Phone: (800) 270-1175 or (760) 323-5806
URL: http://www.somatherapy.com

Földiklinik GmbH & Co. KG
e-Mail: foeldi@foeldiklinik.de
URL: http://www.lymphologie.de
URL: http://www.foeldi@foeldiklinik.de
URL: http://www.foeldischule.de

International Society of Lymphology
Lymphology Journal
Arizona Health Sciences Center
Dept. of Surgery (GS and T)
P.O. Box 245063
Tucson AZ 85724-5063
e-Mail: lymph@u.arizona.edu

Lymphedema Association of Australia
e-Mail: casley@enteret.com.au
URL: http://www.lymphoedema.org.au

Lymphedema Research Foundation
URL: http://www.lymphaticresearch.org

National Lymphedema Network
1611 Telegraph Ave., Suite 1111
Oakland, CA 94612-2138
Support group for patients with lymphedema, clearinghouse for information about lymphedema
Phone: (800) 541-3259
e-Mail: nln@lymphnet.org
URL: http://www.lymphnet.org

Bibliography

Bach, C. S., & Lewis, G. P. (1973). Lymph flow and lymph protein concentration in skin and muscle of the rabbit hind limb. *Journal of Physiology (London), 235*, 477.

Brobeck, J. R. (Ed.) (1979). *Best and Taylor's physiological basis of medical practice* (10th ed.). Baltimore: Williams & Williams.

Burch, S. (1997). *Recognizing health and illness.* Lawrence, KS: Health Positive! Publishing.

Caenar, J. S., Pflug, J. J., Reig, N. O., & Taylor, L. M. (1970). Lymphatic pressures and the flow of lymph. *British Journal of Plastic Surgery, 23*, 305.

Casley-Smith, J. R. (1984). Lymphatic manifesto. *Lymphology, 17*, 109–110.

Chikly, Bruno, M.D. (2001). *Silent waves: The theory and practice of lymph drainage massage.* Scottsdale, AZ: IHH Publishing.

Courtice, F. C. (1986). Has modern technology changed our concept of lymph formation? *Lymphology, 19*, 65.

De Godoy, J. M. P. (2002). Preliminary evaluation of a new, more simplified physiotherapy technique for lymphatic drainage. *Lymphology, 35*, 91–93.

Foldi, E. (1995). Massage and damage to lymphatics. *Lymphology 28*, 1–30.

Froley, H. (1926). Observations of contractility of lacteals. *Journal of Physiology (London), 62*, 267.

Gnepp, D. R., & Sloop, C. H. (1978). The effect of passive motion on the flow and formation of lymph. *Lymphology, 11*, 32.

Grupp, D. R. (1984). Lymphatics. In N. C. Staub & A. E. Taylor (Eds.), *Edema*. New York: Raven.

Guyton, A. C. (1981). *Textbook of medical physiology* (6th ed.). Philadelphia: Saunders.

Hall, J. G., Morris, B., & Wooley, G. (1965). Intrinsic rhythmic propulsion of lymph in the unanaesthetized sheep. *Journal of Physiology, 180*, 1881.

McHale, N. G., & Roddie, I. C. (1976). The effect of transmural pressure on pumping activity in isolated bovine lymphatic vessels. *Journal of Physiology, 261*, 255.

McMaster, P. D. (1937). Changes in the cutaneous lymphatics of human beings in the lymph flow under normal and pathological conditions. *Journal of Experimental Medicine, 65*, 347.

McMaster, P. D. (1946). Conditions in the skin influencing interstitial fluid movement, lymph formation, and lymph flow. *Annals of the New York Academy of Science, 46*, 743.

Mislin, H. (1976). Active contractility of the lymphangion and coordination of the lymphangion chains. *Experientia, 37*, 820.

Mislin, H., & Schipp, H. (1967). Structural and functional relations of the mesenteric vessels. In Ruttiman, A. (ed.), *Progress in lymphology*. Stuttgart: Thieme Verlag.

O'Morchoe, C. C. C., & O'Morchoe, P. J. (1987). Differences in lymphatic and blood capillary permeability: Ultrastructural-functional correlations. *Lymphology, 20*, 205–209.

Olszewski, W. L. (ed.) (1991). *Lymph stasis: Pathophysiology, diagnosis, and treatment.* Boca Raton, FL: CRC Press.

Olszewski, W. L. (2002, September). Continuing discovery of the lymphatic system in the 21st century: A brief overview of the past. *Lymphology, 35*(3), 99–103.

Olszewski, W. L., & Engelset, A. (1979). Lymphatic contractions. *New England Journal of Medicine, 300*, 316.

Olszewski, W. L., & Engelset, A. (1980). Intrinsic contractility of prenodal lymph vessels and lymph flow in the human leg. *American Journal of Physiology, 239*, H775.

Overholser, L., & Moody, R.A. (1988). Lymphatic massage and recent scientific discoveries. *Massage Therapy Journal, 46*, 55–59.

Parsons, R. J., & McMaster, P. D. (1938). The effect of the pulse upon the formation and flow of lymph. *Journal of Experimental Medicine, 68*, 353.

Pullinger, B. D., & Florey, H. W. (1935). Some observations on the structure and function of lymphatics: Their behavior in local edema. *British Journal of Experimental Pathology, 16*, 49.

Reddy, N. P. (1987). Lymph circulation: Physiology, pharmacology, and biomechanics. *CRC Critical Reviews in Biomedical Engineering, 14*, 45.

Ryan, T. J. (1998). *Lymphology*, 128, 129.

Schad, H., & Brechtelsbauer, H. (1978). Thoracic duct lymph flow and composition in conscious dogs and the influence of anesthesia and passive limb movement. *Pfluegers Archives, 371*, 25.

Smith, R. O. (1949). Lymphatic contractility, a possible intrinsic mechanism of lymphatic vessels for transport of lymph. *Journal of Experimental Medicine, 90*, 497.

Taylor, K. (1995). *The ethics of caring.* Santa Cruz, CA: Hanford Mead Publishers.

Wang, G., & Zhong, S. (1985). Experimental study of lymphatic contractility and its clinical importance. *Annals of Plastic Surgery, 15*, 278.

Weissleder, H., & Schuchhardt, C. (eds.). (1997). *Lymphedema diagnosis and therapy.* Bonn: Kagerer Kommunikation.

Werner, R., & Benjamin, B. (1998). *A massage therapist's guide to pathology.* Baltimore: Williams & Wilkins.

White, M. H., Hanto, D., & Witte, C. L. (1977). Clinical and experimental techniques to study the lymphatic system. *Vascular Surgery, 11*, 120.

Witte, C. L., & Witte, M. H. (1987). Contrasting patterns of lymphatic and blood circulatory disorders. *Lymphology 20*, 171–178.

Wittlinger, H., & Wittlinger, G. (1982). *Introduction to Dr. Vodder's manual lymph drainage.* Heidelberg: Haug Verlag.

Wittlinger, H., & Wittlinger, G. (1998). *Textbook of Dr. Vodder's manual lymph drainage* (6th ed.). Heidelberg: Haug Verlag, 18.

Yoffey, J. M., & Courtice, F. C. (1970). *Lymphatics, lymph, and lymphomyeloid complex.* New York: Academic Press.

Zweifach, B. W., & Prather, J. W. (1975). Micromanipulation of pressure in terminal lymphatics in the mesentary. *American Journal of Physiology, 228*, 1326.

Endnotes

[1] Gasparo Asselli described the lymph vessels in a dog in 1622; Johann Vesling observed human lymph vessels in 1624. William Harvey described human blood circulation in 1628.

[2] Chikly, Bruno, M.D., "Silent waves: The theory and practice of lymph drainage therapy," IHH Publishing, Scottsdale, AZ, 2001, 12.

[3] National Lymphedema Network, 21 Post St., Suite 404, San Francisco, CA 94115, http://www.lymphnet.org.

[4] DeGodoy, J. M. P. (2002). Preliminary evaluation of a new, more simplified physiotherapy technique for lymphatic drainage. *Lymphology, 35,* 91–93.

[5] Olszewski, W. L. (ed.). (1991). *Lymph stasis.* 475.

[6] Casley-Smith, J. R. (1984). Lymphatic manifesto. *Lymphology, 17,* 109–110.

[7] Weissleder, H., & Schuchhardt, C. (1997). 264–265.

[8] Olszewski, W. L. (2002, September). Continuing discovery of the lymphatic system in the 21st century: A brief overview of the past. *Lymphology, 35*(3), 100.

[9] Ryan, T. J. *Lymphology, 31* (1998), 128–129.

[10] O'Morchoe, C. C. C., & O'Morchoe, P. J. (1987).

[11] Witte, C. L., & Witte, M. H. (1987).

[12] Casley-Smith (1984).

[13] Reddy (1987).

[14] Hall et al. (1965).

[15] Guyton (1981). 372.

[16] Ryan, T. J. (1998). *Lymphology, 31.* 128–129.

[17] Parsons & McMaster (1938). Caener et al. (1970). Wang & Zhong (1985).

[18] McMaster (1946).

[19] Casley-Smith (1984).

[20] Yoffey & Courtice (1970).

[21] Olszewski, W. L. (2002, September). Continuing discovery of the lymphatic system in the 21st century: A brief overview of the past. *Lymphology, 35*(3), 102–103.

[22] Ibid.

[23] Casley-Smith, J. R. (1984). Lymphatic manifesto. *Lymphology, 17,* 109–110.

[24] Linda Barufaldi, D.C., in private communication with author.

[25] Casley-Smith (1984).

[26] Witte, C. L., & Witte, M. H. (1987). 175.

[27] Foldi, E. Massage and damage to lymphatics. *Lymphology, 28,* 1:1–3.

[28] Werner, R., & Benjamin, B. 225.

[29] Burch, S. 185.

[30] Wittlinger, H., & Wittlinger, G. 73.

[31] Caenar et al. (1970).

[32] Parsons & McMaster (1938).

[33] McMaster (1946).

[34] Olszewski & Engeset (1979).

[35] Wang & Zhong (1985).

[36] J. M. P. de Godoy, F. Batigalia, M. de F. G. Godoy. Preliminary evaluation of a new, more simplified physiotherapy technique for lymphatic drainage. *Lymphology, 35*(2), 91–93.

[37] Ryan, T. J. (1998). *Lymphology,* 128–129.

[38] Wittlinger, H., & Wittlinger, G. (1982).

[39] Wittlinger, H., & Wittlinger, G. (1998).

[40] Mislin (1976).

[41] Olszewski & Engeset (1979 and 1980).

[42] Olszewski & Engeset (1979).

[43] Olszewski, W. L. (ed.). (1991). *Lymph stasis.* 473.

[44] Leichtman, R. (2001). Personal communication to Judy Dean.

Index

Numbers followed by the letter "f" indicate figures.